JOAN WILEN
AND
LYDIA WILEN

SHOES IN THE FREEZER,
BEER IN THE FLOWER BED

And Other Down-Home Tips

(for House and Garden)

A FIRESIDE BOOK

PUBLISHED BY SIMON AND SCHUSTER

FIRESIDE
Rockefeller Center
1230 Avenue of the Americas
New York, NY 10020

FIRESIDE and colophon are registered trademarks
of Simon & Schuster Inc.

Designed by Katy Riegel

Manufactured in the United States of America

1   3   5   7   9   10   8   6   4   2

Library of Congress Cataloging-in-Publication Data

Wilen, Joan.
Shoes in the freezer, beer in the flower bed : and other down-home
tips for house and garden / Joan Wilen and Lydia Wilen.
p.   cm.
Includes index.
1. Home economics.   I. Wilen, Lydia.   II. Title.
TX158.W47   1997
640—dc20   96-30999   CIP

ISBN 0-684-80456-5

CONTENTS

ACKNOWLEDGMENTS

With thanks and love to—

The super people at Simon & Schuster: our patient and supportive editor Cindy Gitter, Trish Todd, and Matt Walker, copyeditor Maggie Cheney, and designer Katy Riegel.

Our always-wonderful agent, Elaine Markson, and Pari Berk, the best follow-upper, and

Marilyn Abraham and Mitch Horowitz for starting it all.

With respect and gratitude to—

Jude C. Williams, Linda Wilen, Robert Weinstein, Judy Twersky, Laura Torbet, Patricia Telesco, Linda Spencer, Rudy Shur, Alison Rhein, D.V.M., Carol Rees, Earl Proulx, Mary Ellen Pinkham, Eileen Nock, Chris Madsen, Peter Lorie, Jeremy Light, Sophie Lasne, Vicki Lansky, Arlen Hollis Kane, Dick Hyman, Sharon Tyler Herbst, Heloise, Hap Hatton, Betty-Anne Hastings, Peter Harper, Wendy Gebb, Andre Pascal Gaultier, Claudia De Lys, Scott Cunningham, Mary-Beth Connors, Peter A. Ciullo, Evelyn Jones Childers, Bob Cerullo, Al Carrell, Dr. Myles H. Bader, Bert Bacharach, Sr., John Amorosso, and Christine Allison.

Special thanks to—

Larry Ashmead for unconditional thoughtfulness.

Nancy Rose and the experts at The New York Botanical Garden,

Harris Publications' publishing director, Phyllis Goldstein,

Jean-Louis Carbonnier and Tiffany Sysum of the Champagne Wines Information Bureau, and

PCSI for servicing our computer.

INTRODUCTION

When we were kids growing up in Brooklyn, we had it made. We never stepped foot into the kitchen. We never had to. Our mother was the world's greatest cook.

When Mom wasn't cooking, she spent a lot of time doing other things domestic, like sewing and cleaning. While cleaning the house wasn't Mom's favorite thing, she seemed to get a lot of satisfaction knowing that, at any given moment, our home could pass the white-glove test. My mother's ultimate compliment after visiting someone else's home was "It's so clean you could eat off the floor."

While Mom was busy cooking and cleaning, our father was fixing and maintaining things. Relatives and neighbors all knew to "Give it to Jack. Jack will fix it." Our dad could fix anything—yes, *anything!*—sometimes he'd fix things even before they broke.

But that was then. When we began the writing of this book, we thought we'd better learn how to do all of this stuff. We looked at each other and asked, "Which way is the kitchen?"

As you will see, we found a kinder, gentler way of cleaning, enabling us to steer clear of ammonia, bleach, kerosene. In other words, we've eliminated all toxic pollutants that can be harmful. Why bother with them if there are safe, inexpensive, practical, and effective alternatives?

So get out the baking soda, vinegar, baking soda, fabric-softener sheets, baking soda, table salt—oh, and don't forget the baking soda. Please God, don't let some study released in the *Journal of the Ameri-*

can Medical Association conclude that baking soda causes something horrible in mice, monkeys, or men.)

As for the kitchen, chances are, neither of us will ever win the Pillsbury Bake-off, but we now know a lot of good tips to make the preparation of food as easy and efficient as possible.

And then there's the garden. Aside from an aloe vera plant, peace lilies, a twenty-year-old ivy plant, and a Chia Pet, here in our New York City apartment, Central Park is our garden. When it came time to write the chapter for the book, we thought it best to turn to the expertise of friends and authorities in the field (no pun intended).

Along with practical down-home hints for house and garden, we've included superstitions that we like to think of as *luck legends.* Don't be surprised at how many *luck legends* are familiar to you, and how many more these bring to mind. We figure that if it doesn't take much effort, it's worth following, doing, or using—if you're so inclined.

Meanwhile, thank you for your interest in our work. We hope this book gives you all kinds of help as it becomes a best-seller—knock wood.

1

GENERAL HOUSEKEEPING

DUSTING

• **What to Use:** In addition to your usual dust rags, dust with used fabric-softener sheets and furniture will be clean and lint-free—and smell good too.

Wear an old pair of cotton gloves or socks on your hands. Polish with one hand and buff with the other.

Dust with discarded shoulder pads. They're soft, they fit comfortably in your palm, and they're washable.

• **Shelves and Drawers:** Don't put a nozzle on the vacuum cleaner hose. Instead, cover the hose opening with a piece of cheesecloth or old pantyhose pulled taut, and secure it in place with a rubber band. Now you're ready to suck up dust from shelves and the insides of drawers without having to empty them first.

• **Venetian Blinds:** Wear cotton gloves or socks on your hands to dust the slats.

If you run fabric-softener sheets over the slats, they should stay cleaner longer, because the sheets help repel dust.

Incidentally, if you need to cover up a stain on a white venetian-blind tape, use white liquid shoe polish.

• **35mm Slides, Negatives:** A blow dryer on the cold-air setting will safely clean the dust off transparencies and negatives.

• **Cleaning a Dust Mop:** The days of shaking a mop out the window are over. Instead, put the dusty mop head in a plastic or paper bag, scrunch up the neck of the bag and hold it tight, then shake-

shake-shake. When you take the mop out of the bag, it should be dust-free.

DUSTING HARD-TO-REACH PLACES

• **Yardstick:** Put an old clean sock or unwearable pair of pantyhose on the end of a yardstick and secure it with string or a rubber band. Then use it for dusting up-highs, unders, and behinds.

• **Hockey Stick:** If you just happen to have a hockey stick lying around, wrap a cloth or towel around the blade (the shorter part of the stick), then secure it with rubber bands or string. It's tops for dusting the top of a door, the tops of picture frames, the top shelf, and hard-to-reach upper wall molding. A golf club will also work well.

• **Broom Handle:** Wrap any kind of tape—sticky side out—around the end of a broom handle, then use it to reach cobwebs in corners. Or attach a nylon net pouf with a rubber band or tack at the top of the broom handle.

• **Long-Handled Auto Snow Brush:** This brush is perfect for hard-to-reach areas like in and around a radiator. It's long and slim enough to fit between the radiator tubes.

WOOD FURNITURE

• **To Remove Old Polish and Dirt:** Put two tea bags in a pot with one quart of water and bring it to a boil. Cool to room temperature, dip a soft cloth in the solution, wring it damp, and wipe furniture

Folk Belief: Spider Webs

If you run into a spider web, wash up—because chances are,

you may expect to meet a friend.

with it. Buff it dry with a soft cloth, then assess whether or not it should be polished.

Wood surfaces will be cleaned and lightly polished after being wiped with a mixture of one teaspoon olive oil and one teaspoon white vinegar in one quart warm water. Use a soft cloth to apply and another one to wipe dry.

• **Make-It-Yourself Furniture Polish:** The general rule with self-made polish is both to rub it in and wipe it off with a soft cloth. Here are two from which to choose: combine ⅓ cup white vinegar with 1 cup olive oil or 3 drops lemon extract with 1 cup mineral oil. Baby oil can be used in place of olive or mineral oil.

• **Fingerprint-Free:** Sprinkle cornstarch on the just-polished furniture and buff with a soft cloth. The cornstarch will make fingerprints disappear as well as absorb excess polish.

• **Restoring Dried-out Furniture:** Dab petroleum jelly on a soft cloth and polish to help feed and restore dry wood. Don't be surprised when you see the wood's grain and natural luster reappear.

• **To Remove Water Marks/Heat Scars/White Rings:** Massage mayonnaise into the marks and leave it on overnight. Next morning, wipe off the mayo, and the marks should be gone. You can also use petroleum jelly, butter, or margarine. For a really stubborn

Folk Belief: Knocking on Wood

Even the least superstitious of us reaches for a nearby piece of furniture,

a bookcase, a cutting board, and——in sheer desperation——our own heads

to knock wood. *It's ingrained in our behavior to do it: knock-knock-*

knock.When? As we're talking about something good in our lives.

Why? So that our good luck will continue.

ring, mix equal amounts of cigarette or cigar ashes with the mayonnaise and repeat the above procedure.

Non-gel white toothpaste is effective in removing water rings from furniture. Dab toothpaste on a damp cotton cloth and gently massage the ring in a circular motion until it's gone. Wipe and buff with a dry cotton cloth.

For a really stubborn ring, mix equal amounts of baking soda and toothpaste and massage, then wipe and buff.

• **To Prevent Water Marks:** With a soft cloth, apply floor wax to furniture and quickly rub it in. It will leave a water-resistant finish on the surface.

• **To Cover a Small Dark Wood Scratch:** Prepare a paste of instant coffee and water and rub it into the scratch. Wipe off the excess, then challenge your friends to find the scratch.

• **To Cover a Small Varnished-Wood Scratch:** Rub the meat of a pecan, walnut, Brazil nut, or peanut into the scratch. If that doesn't do it, try an eyebrow pencil, shoe polish, or a crayon whose color matches that of the wood.

• **To Cover a Small Mahogany Scratch:** Use iodine to fill it in and make it unnoticeable.

• **To Prevent Furniture Scratches:** With glue or double-sided tape, attach felt to the bottoms of vases and other decorative knick-knacks to avoid scratching furniture surfaces.

• **To Prevent Furniture from Scratching the Floor** (see FLOORS in Chapter 3, "Rugs, Carpets, and Floors.")

• **To Remove Adhesive Labels:** A price tag, an identifying label from an auction, or a storage sticker may leave traces of adhesive. Dip a cloth in vegetable oil and gently scrub the area clean.

• **To Remove Decals:** Cover the decal with a cloth that's been soaked in warmed white vinegar. After a few minutes, you should be able to peel or wash off the decal.

WROUGHT-IRON FURNITURE

• **To Cover a Scratch:** Rub a black crayon on the scratch and blend it in with a soft cloth.

UPHOLSTERED FURNITURE

• **General Rule:** Always test an inconspicuous area with whatever you want to use before you use it on a conspicuous area.

• **To Clean:** In a big bowl, combine one part mild detergent with four parts water. Whip the mixture with a whisk, creating lots of foam. Clean the furniture by brushing the foam on the upholstery. Then wipe off the foam, blot it as dry as you can get it, and use a blow dryer to complete the job.

• **To Get Rid of a Musty Smell:** Scatter kitty litter on the upholstery and let it stay there for a few hours, then vacuum.

• **To Get Rid of the Smell of Smoke:** Scatter baking soda on the upholstery and let it stay there for a few hours, then vacuum.

• **To Remove Pet Hair:** Wipe the upholstery with a slightly dampened sponge or chamois cloth.

• **To Remove a Grease Stain:** Rub cornmeal into a stain and leave it overnight. Next morning, vacuum it all away.

Make a paste of three parts baking soda and one part water and massage it into the stain. When it dries, vacuum it away.

• **To Clean Leather Upholstery:** Remove wax buildup by rubbing with a solution of ¼ cup white vinegar and ½ cup water (stale beer also works). Next, wash the leather with saddle soap and water. Then buff back the leather's shine with a soft cloth.

• **To Clean Vinyl Upholstery:** Oil can harden vinyl and make it crack, so be sure to clean vinyl head and arm rests often. Wipe off body oil with a damp sponge sprinkled with baking soda or moistened with vinegar. Then wash the vinyl with watered-down dish detergent.

MIRRORS

• **To Clean Mirrors:** Pour equal parts of water and white vinegar into a bowl, then dip a scrunched-up newspaper page into it. Squeeze out the page, and when it's no longer dripping, wipe the mirror with it over and over. Then, give it a finishing shine by rubbing with a soft cloth, soft paper towel, or dry newspaper.

Use old pantyhose, a lint-free coffee filter, or gift wrapping tissue paper to give mirrors a lint-free shine.

Prepare a cup of tea for yourself and another cup for cleaning a mirror.

• **To Fix a Worn Spot:** Cover that peekaboo area in the reflective backing of the mirror by taping a piece of aluminum foil to the back.

• **Mirror Mist Prevention** (See MIRROR in Chapter 8, "BATHROOM.")

WINDOWS

• **To Clean:** Mix 1 cup white vinegar with 3 cups water. Optional: Add ⅛ cup rubbing alcohol to the mixture for a brighter shine. Dip scrunched-up newspaper pages into the solution, squeeze them dripless, and clean the window. (Wear rubber gloves to keep the newspaper print off your hands.) Dry the window with *dry* scrunched-up newspaper pages. For that brighter-than-bright shine, buff the window with a soft cloth—or better yet, a clean blackboard eraser.

• **Cleaning and Priming:** Mix ¼ cup cornstarch in 1 quart water. Drench a coarse washcloth in the mixture, wring it out, and wash the window with it. Then dry the window with a soft cloth or paper towel. After the first few times you use this process, the window will be primed, so you should be able to just polish with a clean, dry cloth.

• **When to Clean:** If you want less streaking (and who doesn't?), clean windows on an overcast day. They will dry more slowly, giving

Folk Belief: Mirrors

Mirrors are said to deflect evil and attract good. It is customary in many cultures to have an artistic arrangement of mirrors at the entrance of one's dwelling. (It looks good, too.)

you time to wipe them off. On a bright, sunny day, windows will dry before you have a chance to wipe them dry, leaving streaks.

• **Finding Streaks:** Clean from side to side on the outside of the window, and up and down on the inside. That way, if there's a streak, you will know right off which side it's on.

• **To Prevent Frost:** When the weather forecast promises freezing temperatures, moisten a cloth with glycerine and spread a thin layer across the inside of the window.

• **Putting Up/Taking Down Metal Storms and Screens:** To make this seasonal task easier, spray the metal window frames with a nonstick vegetable spray—and trade *struggling* for *gliding.*

GLASS-TOP TABLE

(See WINDOWS above or the remedy below.)
• **To Clean:** Dampen a cloth with a mixture of two teaspoons liquid fabric softener in one pint warm water and wipe the table with it. Dry with a cloth or paper towel for a clean, lint-free surface.

TELEVISION SCREEN

• **To Clean:** Wipe with a cloth moistened with rubbing alcohol.
• **To Dustproof:** Give the screen the once-over with a fabric-softener sheet. Since the sheet helps eliminate static cling, dust will be repelled instead of adhering to the screen.

TELEPHONE

• **To Clean:** Dip a soft cloth in alcohol or white vinegar and scrub that phone spotless. For those hard-to-reach spaces around the buttons, use a dipped cotton swab. The smell disappears in a minute.

IVORY AND BONE:
PIANO OR ORGAN KEYBOARDS

• **The Key to Keys:** Keep a keyboard exposed to the air and light. Circulating air helps prevent warping, and light has a bleaching effect, keeping the keys their whitest.

• **To Clean:** Carefully wipe the keys with a soft cloth and yogurt, milk, rubbing alcohol, one tablespoon hydrogen peroxide in one cup water, two parts salt to one part lemon juice, non-gel toothpaste, or a paste of baking soda and water. Wipe the chosen cleaning agent off with a moist cloth, then buff with a dry one.

CRYSTAL AND GLASS

• **To Clean Crystal or Glass:** As a rule, soak the object in a mixture of two parts white vinegar with three parts water. After about thirty minutes, scrub off the dirt, rinse, and dry it with a lint-free cloth.

• **Narrow-Neck Bottles or Vases:** If you don't have a bottle brush to clean the unreachable bottom and sides of a bottle or vase, use rice to help do the job. Toss in a couple of tablespoons of dry, uncooked grains, along with ¼ cup white vinegar, and shake-shake-shake. The rice scours without scratching while the vinegar cleans.

For an unreachable dirty bottle bottom, drop in 1 or 2 denture-cleaning tablets and ½ to 1 cup water. Shake while it fizzes.

• **To Clean Cruddy Vases:** Prepare a solution of 2 parts strong tea to 1 part white vinegar. (The amount depends on the size of the vase and where the caked-on water line is.) Give the vase at least a day to sit with the solution in it. Then wash (or scour if necessary) with dish detergent, rinse, and dry.

• **To Remove Hard-Water Deposits:** Fill the vase with warm water and add the cut-up rind of a grapefruit. Leave it that way for a day, then wash, rinse, and dry.

WALLPAPER

• **To Clean Dirty Spots:** Wipe stains away with even, up-and-down strokes, using crustless chunks of stale seedless bread or an art-gum eraser.

• **To Remove Fresh Grease Stains:** Blot off as much as possible with a clean paper towel. To lift off the rest of the stain, cover it with a clean paper towel and go over it with a warm (not hot) iron. As the grease transfers onto the paper towel, keep replacing the towel until there's no more grease.

Put a paste of cornstarch and water on the grease spot. Once it dries, brush it off.

• **To Remove Crayon Marks:** Squish non-gel white toothpaste on the marks and leave it for about thirty minutes. Then wipe it off with a dry cloth.

• **To Clean Washable Wallpaper:** Combine ¼ cup liquid dish-washing detergent and 1 cup warm water, then whip it with a hand mixer or rotary beater until you get a stiff foam. Wash the wallpaper with the foam on a sponge or cloth.

METALS

• **General Caution:** Before using any cleaners, polishers, detarnishers, and verdigris removers, first test the solution on an inconspicuous portion of the metallic object. Better safe than *oops!*

• **General Rule:** Damp metal tarnishes really fast, so after cleaning, be sure to dry thoroughly.

• **To Make (Most) Metals Shine:** Rub metal objects with cork.

• **A Polish for Tarnished Metal:** If you have access to a fireplace, collect wood ashes in a jar and add baking soda—two tablespoons baking soda for each cup of ashes. Shake-shake-shake, and it's ready for any tough tarnishing job. To use, add enough water to a scoop of the mixture to form a paste. Rub the paste on the metal with a damp cloth. Then wipe off with a soft cloth, rinse, and dry.

ALUMINUM

• **To Clean:** Rub smooth aluminum with the juicy side of a lemon wedge.

(UNLACQUERED) BRASS OR COPPER

• **To Clean:** Sprinkle salt or baking soda on a wedge of lemon and rub. Remember, salt is a corrosive, so rinse the surface thoroughly with hot water, then buff it dry with a soft cloth.

Dip a damp cloth in Worcestershire sauce and rub tarnish off the brass. Then wipe the sauce off with a damp cloth and buff it dry with a soft cloth.

How does the Navy keep the top brass's brass clean? With powdered fruit juice, like Tang, we've been told. Add enough water to the powder to make a paste and rub it on with a damp cloth. Wipe off with a damp cloth! Rinse! Buff dry! At ease! Dismissed!

Apply non-gel white toothpaste on a damp, soft cloth. Rinse thoroughly and buff dry.

• **To Remove Verdigris:** The green patina or copper chloride or copper sulfate that forms on brass, copper, and bronze can be removed with a paste of lemon juice and baking soda. Apply the paste with a cloth, scour, rinse thoroughly, and buff dry.

BRONZE

• **To Clean :** Mix equal parts of salt and flour, then add enough white vinegar to make a thick paste. With a damp cloth rub the paste on the bronze. Wash thoroughly, rinse, and buff dry.

• **To Remove Verdigris** (see [UNLACQUERED] BRASS OR COPPER above).

CHROME

• **To Clean and Shine:** Take a piece of aluminum foil about six inches by three inches and sculpt it—shiny side out—around the tips of your four fingers (not the thumb), covering the first knuckles. Moisten the foil and rub the chrome with it. You'll know it's working when the foil turns black. Then wipe the chrome with a damp soft cloth.

Rub the chrome with a wedge of lemon or orange juice or rubbing alcohol. Then wipe with a damp soft cloth.

Dampened scrunched newspaper pages rubbed on chrome will shine it and leave it lint-free. This is especially good for chrome-trimmed glass fixtures or furniture, because you can also clean the glass with the wet newspaper.

• **To Remove Rust:** Most rust stains can be rubbed off with a cloth dampened with vinegar.

PEWTER

• **A No-No:** Never wash pewter in an automatic dishwater, because it has a low melting point.

• **To Keep Pewter Clean:** Wash with mild soapsuds and hot water, rinsing until you're sure that there's no more soap film.

Clean pewter by rubbing it with the large, outer leaves of a head of cabbage. Then buff it with a soft cloth.

• **Prevent Tarnish:** Pewter objects will stay untarnished longer if kept in a glass case in a warm area.

• **Detarnishing Antique Pewter:** Dip No. 0000 steel wool in olive oil and gently proceed (with caution) to scour off the tarnish. Once the tarnish has vanished, wash, rinse, and dry with a soft cloth.

• **To Remove Beverage Stains from Pewter Mugs:** Cover the stain with baking soda. Moisten a soft cloth with olive oil or vegetable oil and gently massage the stain away. Then wash, rinse, and dry.

SILVER

• **A Must for Silver Owners:** For good advice, including tips from Tiffany & Company, check out SILVERWARE in Chapter 9, "Kitchen Cleaning."

• **To Clean:** Smear a thin layer of non-gel white toothpaste on silver and place it in a basin of warm water. Gently scour the object with a cloth until most of the toothpaste foams off. Wipe all the toothpaste off, rinse, and buff dry with a soft cloth.

Purée a banana peel in a blender or food processor. Yes, the peel—without the hard ends, of course. Massage the puréed peel onto the silver, then wipe it off, rinse, and buff dry with a soft cloth.

If you have a carton of milk that's gone sour, pour it in a basin and soak tarnished silver in it for about thirty minutes. Then wash the silver with a mild detergent, rinse, and buff dry with a soft cloth.

The following remedy, as popular as it seems to be with the gurus of grime, requires enough warnings and has enough variations to make us wonder if it's worth it. But here it is anyway, with thanks to Heloise for her version: Put aluminum foil—shiny side up—on the bottom of a heatproof glass bowl (Pyrex is perfect). Lay the silver object in the bowl, add one heaping tablespoon baking soda, then pour in enough just-boiled, scalding hot water to cover the object. Within minutes, the tarnish will collect on the foil. When it looks like the job is done, carefully remove the silver item, rinse it thoroughly, and buff it dry with a soft cloth.

• **Warning:** This cleaning method removes dark accents in design crevices, which isn't always a good thing. It can also soften the cement of hollow-handled flatware. While it may take off tarnish quickly without rubbing, it usually leaves silver with a lackluster finish. For these reasons, this method should only be used occasionally—or not at all—on heirloom pieces.

Folk Belief: Silver Outside

One New Year's Eve, right before you go to bed, place a piece of silver outside. Next morning, if you bring the silver back inside without speaking to anyone first, you'll be financially set for the entire year. (For apartment dwellers, you might want to tape a piece of silver on your windowsill.)

• **To Brighten:** Dip a piece of raw potato in baking soda and rub the silver, then wipe and buff dry with a soft cloth. A paste of baking soda and water will do the same thing.

• **To Prevent Tarnish:** In cases or cabinets that house silver, inconspicuously scatter pieces of blackboard chalk or charcoal briquettes to absorb moisture.

• **Storing No-Nos:** Keep rubber, as in rubber bands, away from silver. It can corrode it.

Do not wrap silver in newspaper. It's too acidic and will promote tarnish.

Oak contains acids that are not agreeable to silver. Don't store silver in oak drawers or cabinets.

• **To Prevent Tarnish During Storage:** Cleaned and polished silver must be kept dry and away from air. Ideally, you should wrap silverware in specially treated tarnish-proof bags or nontarnishing tissue paper (available at hardware stores). Also available are bags made of "Pacific" cloth, which are very effective in preventing tarnish. Second best is plastic bags. Remember, don't secure them with rubber bands. And always store silver in a cool, dry place.

CANDLEHOLDERS

• **To Clean Off Wax:** Put the holder in the freezer for about an hour, long enough for the dripped-on wax to freeze, so you can break or peel it off.

If the candleholder won't fit in your freezer, put the dripped-on portion under the faucet and let very hot water run over it until the wax softens enough to be coaxed off with your fingers.

ARTIFICIAL FLOWERS

• **To Dust:** Use a hair dryer on the lowest setting to blow dust off artificial flowers. For delicate dried flowers, use an empty atomizer or turkey baster to puff off the dust.

• **To Clean Fabric Flowers:** Pour one cup salt in a paper or plastic bag that's big enough for the flowers. Then put the flowers in—blossoms first. Hold the neck of the bag closed around the stems, and shake vigorously. Take the flowers out of the bag and shake off all remaining salt over a sink. The flowers should be clean—and look more vivid.

• **To Brighten Plastic Flowers:** After washing them with a mild detergent in warm water, dry them thoroughly. Then spray them with hair spray (a pump spray rather than the aerosol kind that's bad for your lungs and the environment). Or paint on a coat or two of colorless nail polish.

2

GENERAL MAINTENANCE

TOOLS

• **To Prevent Rust:** Clean tools with steel wool, then rub on a thin coat of petroleum jelly.

Keep a charcoal briquette and/or pieces of chalk in your toolbox to absorb moisture.

NUTS, BOLTS, AND SCREWS

• **To Remove:** If you want to remove a nut, bolt, or screw, but it just won't budge, *first* try tightening it a tiny bit, *then* try to undo it.

Carbonated soda—particularly cola—poured on a rusted or just plain stubborn nut or bolt has been known to loosen it.

If there seems to be a lot of rust, douse the nut or bolt with iodine, wait five minutes, then loosen it. If you don't have iodine, use hydrogen peroxide.

• **Got a Screw Loose? Is It Attached to a Knob?** Dip the threaded part of the screw into colorless nail polish, then twist the screw back into its hole. When the polish dries, chances are that screw will be there for the duration. A variation on this remedy is to drip a drop or two of nail polish into the hole, then screw in the screw.

• **Screw Screws Easier:** Screw a screw into a cake of soap, then notice how much easier it will be to work with.

• **Don't Lose Screws:** After you've taken something apart and before you put it back together, put the nuts, bolts, and screws on a thick piece of tape. That way, they won't separate from each other and get lost.

NAILS

• **Out-of-the-Way Spots:** If you have to hammer a nail into an awkward, out-of-the-way spot, let a strip of clay hold the nail for you as you hammer away. Once the nail is in, peel off the clay.

MAKESHIFT CLAMPS

Plastic or wood spring-type clothespins are very inexpensive and handy to have as clamps when puttering around the house.

SCISSORS

• **To Sharpen:** Tear off three pieces of aluminum foil, put them on top of each other, then cut the layered foil at least a dozen times with your dull pair of scissors. Cut a regular piece of paper and see if the scissors are sharp enough. If not, repeat the procedure.

Buff the edges of dull scissors with a steel-wool pad.

As a last resort for an old if-this-doesn't-make-it-better-I'm-going-to-get-rid-of-them pair of scissors, use the scissors to cut a sheet of fine sandpaper several times. This scissors-sharpening method is *not recommended* for a good pair of sewing shears.

Folk Belief: A Rusty Nail

Finding a nail, especially a rusty one, brings good luck. To maximize

the luck, pound the nail into your kitchen door.

• **To Remedy Sticking:** Scissors that stick may need to be lubri-cated. Drops of oil are a no-no, because the oil will get on everything that you cut. Instead, use your own natural oil. Carefully massage the blades with your fingers. Chances are it will make a difference.

BATTERIES

• **Longer Life:** Keep batteries in the refrigerator and you'll prolong their life.

• **Power Boost:** Give old batteries a burst of energy by putting them in the sun for a day.

FUSE BOX

• **Locating a Fuse:** You'll never have to go stumbling through the dark again looking for a fuse if you just tape one on the inside of the fuse box. Don't forget to replace it after you use it.

LIGHTBULBS

• **To Remove a Broken Bulb:** When part of a burned-out light-bulb remains in the socket, turn off the switch, take a bar of soap, jab it into the jagged edges at the base of the bulb, and unscrew it coun-terclockwise.

Instead of the bar of soap, use a cork.

Instead of the cork, use a rubber ball.

Instead of the rubber ball, use a rolled-up magazine.

ELECTRIC CORDS

• **To Organize:** Keep appliance and extension cords untangled in cardboard paper-towel and toilet-tissue tubes. Then, if you're going that far you might consider writing on the tube the length of each cord and the appliance it fits.

BROOM

• **When Shopping for a Broom:** Look for a broom that has a hole in the handle, so that when it's not in use you can hang it up to prevent the bristles from curling. If you have a broom that's unhangable, drill a hole in the top of the broomstick, put cord through it, and hang it up.

• **To Prep a New Broom:** Soak the bristles of a new broom in hot salt water for a few hours before you use it for the first time. It should make the broom last longer.

• **To Clean:** About once a month, clean a broom by dipping it in warm water and letting it air-dry.

FIREPLACE

• **Warning:** Never burn colored newspapers or magazines in the fireplace. They contain lead, which, when airborne, can be very dangerous, especially for children.

• **Soot Reducer:** Cut down on the amount of soot in your fireplace by throwing salt on the fireplace logs every few weeks.

• **Soot Smell Absorber:** Once you've cleaned out the ashes from your fireplace, place a shallow pan of baking soda inside. It should absorb the smell of soot.

Folk Belief: Brooms

Do not bring your old broom into a new house. To stack the deck in your favor when you move into that new house, bring a new broom—and also a loaf of bread to make sure that food is in abundance, salt ensuring you the spice of life, and a candle for light and warmth.

Folk Belief: The Fireplace

When family and friends are gathered around the fireplace, have each one

write out a wish on a piece of paper. Throughout the evening, toss each

person's wish into the fire. If the piece of paper is sucked up the

chimney, the wish should come true soon.

• **To Clear Chimney Soot:** Prepare French-fried potatoes, mashed potatoes, potato latkes, or whatever it takes to gather a whole lot of potato peels. Dry them and then burn them in your fireplace. They burn with a tremendous amount of energy—enough to send the soot up and out the chimney.

• **To Lessen the Mess when Cleaning:** Using a plant mister or spray bottle filled with water, gently spritz the ashes in the inner hearth. Damp ashes will not fly all around the room as you sweep them out.

• **To Clean Glass Fireplace Doors:** Take some of the wood ashes, add a little water, sponge it on the glass, then rinse it off. The dirt should come off with it.

DOORS

• **When a Door Sticks:** Locate the exact spot that's causing the door to stick and sandpaper it down. If the door rubs on the bottom, for instance, wedge coarse sandpaper between the floor and the door, and work the door back and forth until the spot is smoothed out.

• **Quieting Squeaky Hinges:** Spritz door hinges with nonstick vegetable spray or dab on petroleum jelly.

FLOORS

• **Squeaky Hardwood Floors:** Sweep talcum powder back and forth over the squeaky floorboards until all the cracks are filled in and you have peace and quiet.

When the squeaking is caused by nails that have come loose in the floorboards, simply hammer them down. If you have carpet or linoleum covering the floor, and you don't want to pick it up in order to hammer down the nails, place a piece of wood over the floor covering to protect it, then hammer the wood. Chances are, the loose nails two layers below will be nailed down.

DRAWERS

• **Easy Gliding:** Keep drawers gliding in and out easily by going over the tracks or runners with a cake of soap or candle wax.

LOCK AND KEY

• **Locking and Unlocking Made Easy:** Give your key a spritz with nonstick vegetable spray for smoother locking.
• **To Unstick a Lock:** Inject one small puff of talcum powder into the keyhole.
• **To Lubricate a Lock:** With the point of a soft lead pencil, rub the serrations and the underside of the lock's key. Then, insert the key in the lock, move it back and forth, and take it out. Repeat until just about all of the graphite has been transferred from the key into the lock.

WINDOW FRAMES

• **To Stop Rattling:** Attach a couple of self-stick felt corn pads (found in drugstore *foot-aid* sections) to a rattling window frame, and rejoice in the silence.

IS IT ON THE LEVEL?

If you want to know whether or not an object is standing level and you don't have a level, you can make do with a measuring cup that has the same measurement markings on each side of the cup. Fill the cup with water to one of the marks and stand it on the object in question. The water level should be the same on each side of the cup. If it isn't, then the object is not level.

FAUCET DRIP TIP

Wrap a hand towel around a dripping faucet and keep it in place with a rubber band. That way, until you have it fixed, the sound of the drip won't be like the water-torture treatment. Actually, all you may need is a sponge under the drip to make it noiseless.

FOAM-CUSHION COVERS

• **Ease the Casing:** If you've ever laundered cushion covers, you know how hard they are to put back on foam cushions, especially if there's a little bit of shrinkage. Solve the problem by encasing the foam cushion in plastic from a dry cleaner's bag, then put the cushion cover on over it. Do that, and the term *slipcover* will have new meaning.

CANE (WICKER) CHAIRS

• **To Prevent Yellowing:** Sponge down new natural-colored wicker furniture with a mild salt water solution to prevent it from turning yellow.
• **To Firm a Sagging Seat:** The seat of a sagging cane-bottom chair can be firmed by shrinking it. Turn bottoms up and wet the seat's underside with hot water. Let the chair dry naturally, ideally in the sun. If that's not possible, blow-dry it, using a warm—not hot—setting. If the seat isn't as tight as it could be, repeat the entire process.

CABINET MAGNETS

• **To Adjust:** If you have magnet catches on cabinet or armoire door that are really hard to open, weaken the magnetic pull by coverin the magnet with a strip of tape.

OUTDOOR STEPS, WALKWAYS, DRIVEWAYS, SIDEWALKS

• **To De-ice:** Baking soda to the rescue! Sprinkle it on to melt the ic and help prevent slipping. The beauty of baking soda is that it's harm less to shoe soles, ground covering outdoors, and, in case it get tracked in, it can help clean your floors indoors.

SNOW SHOVELS

• **To Make Shoveling Easier:** As soon as the weather turns cold coat your snow shovel with floor wax. It will prevent the shovel from rusting and snow will glide right off.

If you don't prepare the shovel in advance, right before using it coat it with a nonstick vegetable spray, let it dry completely, and ge on with your nonstick shoveling.

OUTDOOR PLASTIC FURNITURE

• **To Keep Clean and Prevent Fading:** A protective coating c car wax will help furniture stay clean and prevent fading from th sun.

3

RUGS, CARPETS,
AND FLOORS

REMOVAL OF STAINS AND STUFF

• **General Rules:** Thoroughly blot up as much of the stain as possible with paper towels. If it's available, use a rolling pin on top of the paper towels to help. Also, clear out all the solid stuff from a spill before trying any stain remedies.

Do not rub a stain. Rubbing embeds the stain deeper into the fiber.

When wiping or rinsing the stained area of a rug, don't get it too wet. Wring out a washcloth or sponge before using it.

• **Fresh Stains:** A spritz of shaving cream can help remove rug stains. Sponge off the shaving cream with water, seltzer, or club soda.

Did someone say seltzer or club soda? Pour either one on a fresh stain. Let it stay there for a minute or two, then sponge it up.

If you like the dry approach to spot removal, try massaging a stain with a slice of two-day-old white bread, then vacuum up the crumbs.

• **Tough Old Stains:** Mix three tablespoons white vinegar and two tablespoons liquid laundry detergent in a quart of water. Wash the stains with this solution, then blot dry.

• **Candle Wax:** Put ice cubes in a plastic bag and hold it against the drippings so that the wax gets brittle and you can pull or break it off. Or go the opposite way with *heat.* Put a brown paper bag on the wax and cautiously place a warm iron on it for a few seconds, long enough to soften the wax and coax it off.

- **Chewing Gum** (See *cold* CANDLE WAX remedy, above.)
- **Coffee:** Blot up as much as possible, then quickly sponge it with cold water. Or mix two tablespoons baking soda and one tablespoon borax in a pint of water. Sponge stains with this solution and blot dry.
- **Crayon Marks:** Press transparent tape against the crayon marks and remove it.
- **Fruit:** Pick up all the pieces of fruit and blot up the fruit juice. Act quickly so that the stains don't have time to set. Use the formula for TOUGH OLD STAINS (above) to sponge on the area, then let the rug dry.
- **Grease, Oil:** Blot up as much as possible, then pour cornmeal or cornstarch on the stain and let it set overnight, then vacuum.
- **Mud:** Scatter cornstarch on the muddied rug and leave it for at least thirty minutes, then vacuum.
- **Red Wine:** After blotting the red wine with a paper towel, neutralize it with white wine, then rub it with a cold, damp washcloth. If that doesn't work, or if you don't have white wine, cover the stain with salt or baking soda. Leave it on overnight and vacuum the spot clean in the morning. If it's not clean, take a cold, damp washcloth and rub-a-dub-dub.
- **Pet Urine:** As soon as you get a puppy, test a tiny patch of every rug in your home with white vinegar. If the vinegar bleaches out the color of any of the rugs, do not use this remedy when the puppy has an accident on it.

Folk Belief: Spilled Wine

According to ancient beliefs, spilling wine is a sign of imminent danger.

Instead of whining about it, dispel the danger by dabbing a drop

of the spilled wine in an invulnerable spot—behind each ear—

with the middle finger of the right hand.

Keep watch for such accidents, because it's important to get to them quickly. Since animals are known to make repeat performances in the same places, it's also important to eliminate the odor—instead of just covering it up—to discourage the pet from returning to those places for the wrong reason. Here's how: Blot up as much of the urine as possible as soon as possible. Mix ½ cup white vinegar with ½ cup water, and sponge it into the fibers. Let it sit for a few minutes, then, once again, blot off as much moisture as possible. If you have the time and the patience, repeat the procedure. If not, go straight to the next step, which is to cover the area with equal parts of salt and baking soda. Let it dry that way for a few hours, then vacuum.

DEODORIZE RUGS, CARPETS

Sprinkle baking soda on the rug the night before you vacuum. When you vacuum up the baking soda, the smell of smoke and other musty odors should disappear. If you forget to prep the rug before you go to bed, sprinkle baking soda and wait at least thirty minutes, then vacuum. It may not be as effective, but then again, it may be.

PET HAIRS

The vacuum may need a little help in picking up pet hairs. First sweep the rug with a damp broom to pick up and/or loosen the hair, then complete the job by vacuuming.

BRIGHTEN RUGS, CARPETS

Sprinkle salt, borax powder, or baking soda on a rug, and leave it there for at least thirty minutes, then vacuum. The salt, borax, or baking soda should brighten the rug—and may also help destroy moth larvae.

THE SWEET SMELL OF . . . WHATEVER

Put a few drops of your favorite light, easy-to-live-with scent—a flowery perfume, cinnamon or strawberry oil, vanilla extract—on a couple of cotton balls. Vacuum them up, then vacuum the rug. The entire room will have that lovely smell.

CLEANING AND THEN SOME

On occasion, sweep your rug with a broom to loosen embedded dirt. Then let the vacuum make a clean sweep of it.

PREVENT THROW RUGS FROM MOVING

Sew a rubber ring—the kind used on Mason jars—on the underside corners of the rug, and it should help the rug stay put.

DRY-CLEAN THROW RUGS

Throw your throw rugs in a dryer on a no-heat setting and let it run for its usual cycle. They come out cleaner; they look better; and it sure beats beating them.

PREVENT STATIC SHOCKS

Keeping a bowl of water in a carpeted room is said to prevent static shocks. If that doesn't work . . .

Mix three tablespoons liquid fabric softener and one cup water in a spray bottle and *lightly* mist the carpet. If you go too heavy on the spray, the mixture will cause dirt to stick to the carpet. Wait till the carpet dries before testing it.

REMOVE "MOVE" INDENTATIONS

There are two approaches to removing indentations caused by moving furniture: hot and cold.
• **Hot:** Cover the indentation with a damp towel, and gently iron the towel (on a low setting). Stop when the towel is dry. You should be able to brush the carpet fibers back to their original place.

• **Cold:** Put an ice cube on the matted area. Leave it overnight. By morning, the moisture from the melted cube should have plumped up the fibers.

MOTHS AND SILVERFISH

Moths and silverfish are repelled by printer's ink. Put a layer of newspapers between the rug and the pad, and you'll have no more bugs snug in your rug.

FLOORS

WOOD FLOORS

• **To Clean:** Mix ½ cup apple cider vinegar in 1 gallon water. Dunk a sponge mop in the solution, wring it out completely, and mop the floor with it, one small area at a time. Follow by buffing the area with a soft cloth.

• **To Clean a Waxed Floor:** Add ¼ cup white vinegar to 1 gallon water, and sponge-mop the floor with this solution. The dirt will come off; the wax will stay on.

• **To Prevent Scratched Floors:** Glue pieces of carpet—pile side down—felt, or self-stick bunion pads on the bottom of furniture legs, such as those on dining-room chairs, to prevent them from scratching the floor as people sit on and get up from them.

When moving furniture, put old socks on the legs to prevent scratching the floor and to make the furniture a lot easier to move. Or cut off the bottom halves of milk and/or juice cartons, wash and dry them, then use them as coasters for furniture feet.

• **To Remove Heel Marks:** Scrub heel marks off a hardwood floor with toothpaste on an old toothbrush, then wipe with a damp sponge or cloth.

Scuff marks will disappear if you wipe them with a little bit of petroleum jelly or baby oil on a cloth. Wipe the area afterward with a paper towel, until there's no trace of that slippery stuff.

• **To Remove a Grease Mark:** If grease drips on a wood floor, put an ice cube or ice-cold water on the spill. When the grease hardens, carefully scrape it off with a knife or spatula.

• **To Sweep up Broken Glass:** Do a clean sweep with a wet broom. The wet end will help pick up shards of glass you may not be able to see.

VINYL OR LINOLEUM

• **To Remove Heel Marks:** Sprinkle baking soda on the marks and rub them with a damp sponge.

A pencil eraser is also effective at erasing heel marks.

• **To Shine Between Waxings:** Mop with a mixture of ½ cup of liquid fabric softener in 1 gallon of water.

• **To Remove Tar:** Without scratching the flooring, carefully scrape the tar with the dull edge of a knife to get as much off as possible. Then rub butter or margarine over the tar that's left. Again, carefully scrape the rest of it off, and wipe with a dry cloth or paper towel.

CERAMIC-TILE FLOOR

• **To Clean:** Dampen a sponge mop with a mixture of ¼ cup white vinegar in 1 gallon water. Run the mop over the ceramic tile. This solution cleans the floor without leaving a film.

4

PAINTING AND WALLPAPER

RIGHT BEFORE YOU START TO PAINT

• **To Protect Your Exposed Skin:** Apply a thin coat of moisturizer, cold cream, shaving cream, or petroleum jelly to your face, neck, hands, and any other body part that may be splattered with paint.

• **If You're Bespectacled:** Prevent your glasses from being bespeckled. Cover each lens with plastic wrap if you're going to wear glasses while painting. Actually, whether your need them or not, it's a good idea to wear glasses or goggles to protect your eyes from splatters, especially when you're painting a ceiling.

• **To Protect Your Hair:** Wear a shower cap, swim cap, paper bag, or plastic Baggie. If hats aren't your thing, wrap plastic wrap around your head to cover your hair.

• **To Protect Your Watch:** Wrap plastic wrap around your watch— or remove it while you paint.

• **To Protect Your Shoes:** Wear a stretched-out pair of socks over them. Shoes with socks over them may be slippery on a waxed floor. When you're painting, you should have some kind of tarp or paper covering the floor, protecting it and making it less slippery. In any case, be careful!

• **To Protect Your Clothes:** Even though you'll be wearing old I-don't-care-if-I-get-paint-on-'em clothes, you can keep the paint drips and smears down to a minimum by wearing a do-it-yourself smock. It's the ol' big plastic trash bag in which you cut holes for your head and arms. It's easy to make and comfortable to wear.

PREPARING THE ROOM

• **To Protect Doorknobs:** Cover them with aluminum foil or plastic wrap, or put plastic sandwich bags over them.
• **When You Take Furniture Knobs Off:** Put matchsticks in the empty screw holes of furniture that you're going to paint, so the holes don't get filled up with paint.
• **To Protect Door and Cabinet Hinges:** Apply petroleum jelly to the hinges. Then you can easily wipe off any paint that gets on them.
• **To Protect Windows:** Cover windowpanes with wet newspaper pages, so that when you paint around them, the glass will remain splatter-free.
• **To Protect the Baseboard:** If you don't want to paint the room's baseboard, cover the baseboard with tape. "Painter's tape," available at hardware and paint stores, is perfect for the job. After the room is painted, it's easier to take off the tape than to remove paint splatters.

PREPARING THE PAINTBRUSH

• **Before You Begin:** Comb the paintbrush several times to get rid of the brush's loose bristles. Nobody likes a hairy wall.
• **Softening a Stiff Paintbrush:** You can bring an old, stiff paintbrush back to life by soaking it in hot vinegar or boil it in a mixture of ½ cup vinegar, ½ gallon water, and 1 cup baking soda.
• **For Lengthier Paint Jobs:** If you don't complete your oil or latex paint job in one day, save yourself the trouble of cleaning the paintbrush. Instead, wrap it in aluminum foil and place it in the freezer. The next day, thaw it out for at least an hour before you go back to work.
• **Painting with a Roller and Tray:** Line the roller tray with aluminum foil, plastic wrap, or a piece of a plastic trash bag. When you're finished painting, discard the foil or plastic, and you won't have to clean the tray.

PREPARING A CAN OF PAINT

• **If Neatness Counts:** With double-sided tape or glue, attach a big paper plate to the bottom of the paint can. It will catch the drips and prevent the bottom of the can from sticking to the floor, a tarp, a ladder's pail rest, or whatever else the can sits on.

• **To Minimize Paint Loss and Dripping:** Carefully drill or punch a few holes in the rim of the paint can. As you wipe the brush against the rim, the excess paint will flow through the holes back into the can. When you place the lid on the can, the holes will be covered, preventing the paint from drying out.

• **To Stir:** A nonstick kitchen utensil makes a great paint stirrer. Try one with holes, such as a draining spoon or skimmer.

• **When Using Roller and Tray:** Put masking or Scotch tape around the entire rim of the can before you pour paint out of it into the tray. Remove the tape to close the just-like-new can.

USING LEFTOVER PAINT

• **To Get Rid of the Skin:** If a layer of skin is on the surface of the paint you want to use, get a large widemouthed jar, stretch a piece of nylon stocking across the opening, and secure it with a rubber band, then strain the paint by pouring it into the jar through the nylon.

Folk Belief: Ladders

While walking under a ladder is not considered lucky, climbing a ladder

with an odd number of rungs is thought to be very lucky. And if you

do walk under a ladder, you may counteract the negative energy by crossing

the fingers of your left hand.

PUTTING AWAY LEFTOVER PAINT

• **To Record Paint Level:** Before you put away a partly used can of paint, use a thick, dark marker to draw a line on the outside of the can that shows—at a glance—how much paint is left inside.

• **Out-of-Sight Skin:** After a while, a skin forms on the surface of a partly used can of paint. To avoid this, make sure the lid is on tight, then store the can upside down. Next time you use the paint, the layer of skin will have formed on the bottom, out of your way.

• **To Prevent Skin from Forming:** If you want to avoid a paint skin problem altogether, just cut a circle of wax paper or aluminum foil the size of the can's diameter, place it on top of the paint, and close the can.

PAINTING DOORS

• **Getting to the Bottom:** Save yourself the job of taking a door off its hinges to paint the bottom of the door. Simply use a toothbrush to do it.

PAINTING STAIRS

• **Having Access while Painting:** Paint every other step of a staircase. When those steps dry, paint the others. That way, people will be able to use the stairway at any given time, even in the midst of your paint job.

Folk Belief: The Steps

If someone falls up the stairs, call the caterer.

There will be a wedding in the house.

PAINTING CLOSETS

• **The Lighter, the Better:** Brighten a lightless closet by painting the inside with white enamel paint.

PAINTING RADIATORS

• **To Help Paint Adhere:** When metal is warm (not hot), paint sticks to it more efficiently. So heat up the radiator a little before you paint it.

PAINTING AN OBJECT

• **To Prevent Sticking:** When you or a child paints an object, you probably place it on newspaper. But what always happens? The object sticks to the newspaper. Use wax paper underneath instead of newspaper. Don't have wax paper? Coat paper with wax by rubbing a candle on the paper, then place the just-painted object on it.

PAINT SMELL

• **Reducing the Scent:** Oil-based paint is strong and hard to take. It may help to mix in one tablespoon vanilla extract to one gallon paint.
• **After Painting:** In each newly painted room, leave a bowl or two of water in a place where it won't be knocked over.

Fill a tray, platter, cookie pan, or a couple of dinner plates with salt, and leave them around the room.

Cut a large yellow onion in quarters and place the chunks around the room.

REMOVING—OOPS!—PAINT SPOTS

• **To Clean Windows or Tile:** Hot white vinegar will remove the paint.

Nail-polish remover will also remove paint from windows or tile. A little dab will do. Let it sink in for a minute or two, then, with a cloth, rub it off.

• **To Clean Windows:** Scrape dried paint off windows with the rim of a penny.

• **To Clean Skin:** Get those fresh paint spots off your skin by rubbing it with shaving cream, baby oil, or olive oil.

• **To Clean Hair:** Rub the spots with baby or olive oil, then comb and shampoo.

PAINTING OUTDOORS

• **When to Get Started:** Tomorrow's the day you're going to paint the outside of your house. You'll get up real early and . . . *wrong!* Don't start painting until the morning dew has had a chance to evaporate completely.

• **To Prevent Insects from Sticking:** Stir one tablespoon citronella into each gallon of paint. Mix well. It should repel insects from the wet paint.

PAINTING WROUGHT-IRON FURNITURE

You'll save time and avoid ruining paintbrushes if you paint wrought-iron (most likely "garden") furniture by dabbing on paint with a sponge.

WALLPAPER

REMOVING OLD WALLPAPER

Prepare a solution of one part liquid fabric softener or laundry starch or two parts hot water. Saturate a sponge with the mixture and wipe the wallpaper with it or apply it with a paint roller. (Or you may prefer to put the solution in a spray bottle and spritz it on.) Once the entire wallpapered area is done, wait twenty minutes for the liquid to do its stuff, then peel off the paper.

PAPERING THE KITCHEN OR BATHROOM

• **Prevent Peeling:** Paint wallpaper seams with clear varnish to help prevent them from peeling in steamy and heated rooms like the kitchen or bathroom.

PREPARING PROPER PATCHES

• **For a Patch Down the Road:** If you have a wall that's not in public sight, tack a piece of leftover wallpaper onto it, so that if you need a patch later, it will be the same color as the paper already on the wall. If you use wallpaper that's left on the roll, after a while, it will be brighter than the somewhat faded paper that's been exposed to light and air.

FOR NEXT TIME

• **For Your Records:** Make note of all the tools and supplies you needed to paper the room, particularly the number of wallpaper rolls used. Put this information in a place where you will find it when you're ready to repaper the room, such as in back of a picture hanging in that room or in a computer file.

5

CLOSETS AND STORAGE AND
BOOK MAINTENANCE

CLOSETS

• **For Fresh-Smelling Closets:** Never keep clothing that needs to be cleaned or laundered in a closet.

Wash the bare floor of a closet with a solution of ½ cup white vinegar and ¼ cup baking soda in a gallon of warm water.

• **Musty Odors and Moisture:** Absorb them away with an open box of baking soda on the closet floor. It works in the fridge: why not in a closet?

Place some charcoal briquettes or cedar chips in a pie tin on the closet floor or in a nylon stocking hanging in the closet to absorb mustiness and moisture.

• **To Get Rid of Mothball Smell:** Place kitty litter in a pie tin or nylon stocking in the closet.

Open a small can of fresh coffee grounds (about 8 ounces) and leave it in the closet until the smell of mothballs or any other unpleasant odor disappears.

• **For Excess Moisture:** Put a rubber band around a few pieces of chalk and put another rubber band around a few more pieces of chalk. Hang the clumps of chalk on each side of the closet to absorb moisture. The bigger the closet, the more chalk you'll probably have to use.

• **For a Sweet-Smelling Closet:** Tape fabric-softener sheets on the walls or under shelves. Make sure the sheets do not touch clothes.

Hang a pomander ball in the closet. It not only smells good, it also repels moths. To make an orange-spice pomander you'll need:

      1 thin-skinned orange (the peel stays on)
      1 box of whole cloves
      1 ounce ground orrisroot
      1 ounce ground cinnamon
      ½ ounce ground nutmeg
      2 feet ¼–½-inch ribbon cut in half

Take one of the pieces of ribbon and tie it around the orange, knotting it on top. Do the same with the other piece of ribbon, and you should have an orange that's encased by ribbon tied on top and crisscrossed on bottom. Nonslippery ribbon such as grosgrain is best, but if you use silky ribbon, you may want to stick a pushpin in on each of the strips around the orange to keep them from slipping. Stick the cloves all over the orange, but not in the ribbon. Place it in a bowl with orrisroot, cinnamon, and nutmeg, and leave it there for four to five days, turning it occasionally. Then, over the sink, with a blow dryer on a cool setting, whoosh away the ground herb powder and hang it in the closet.

STORAGE AND MAINTENANCE

CLOTHES STORAGE

• **To Cover Clothes:** Have you ever found a yellow spot on an article of clothing that appeared inexplicably? It's probably from a polyethylene (plastic dry cleaning) bag. Polyethylene emits a gas that can

Folk Belief: Found Money

When you take your winter coat out of storage, put it on and check the pockets for money. If you find any coins, your business deals will prosper throughout the season.

change the color of clothes or cause spots. If you do not have a *safe* garment bag, use a pillowcase to cover clothes you want to store. Just cut a small hole on top for the hanger to stick through.

• **Mothball Substitute:** When storing winter woolens, you can use whole cloves (the kind used in cooking hams) to repel moths. It does a good job and smells a lot better than mothballs.

• **Storage Bins:** There are wonderful plastic garbage cans readily available in several sizes and reasonably priced. They make great storage bins for clothing. You don't have to bother with moth repellents if you can get cans with airtight covers in which to store freshly laundered or dry-cleaned clothes.

Cashmere sweaters and woolen accessories can be safely stored in large glass jars with some whole cloves wrapped in a nylon stocking.

BOOKS

• **To Prevent Mustiness:** Keep books close to the front of shelves to allow air to circulate. The air will help prevent mustiness.

• **To Dust Books:** Use a wide paintbrush for the job.

• **To Prepare Books for Storage:** If you have to put books away (after all, who has enough shelf space to keep all of their books out?), be sure to store them in a cool, dry place. To prevent mustiness and mildew, wrap charcoal briquettes in cheesecloth or in an old sock and put them in the box, too.

• **To Cure Mustiness:** We all know the smell of an old book. Feh! But you *can* get rid of that musty smell. Crinkle newspaper pages, put them in a big brown bag with the musty book, and close the bag

Folk Belief: Moths

If you spot a moth in your home at night, check your mailbox next morning

for an important piece of mail. (Then check your sweater for holes.)

tightly with a rubber band. After a day or two, check on the book. If the musty smell isn't gone, change the newspaper and close the bag again. Repeat the procedure until the book is completely odor-free. You can also try using a cup of kitty litter instead of newspaper.

If you have a special book that is any of the 3Ms—moldy, mildewed, or musty—use a soft toothbrush to brush off the mold and mildew, then sprinkle cornstarch between the pages and leave it there overnight. Next morning, gently brush out the cornstarch. Some people prefer baking soda instead of cornstarch, but both seem to do the job.

SLEEPING BAG

• **To Store:** Ready to put away your sleeping bag for the season? When you pack it up, put in a few fabric-softener sheets. When you next use it, the sleeping bag will smell like springtime.

BLANKETS

• **To Store:** When closet space is limited, consider storing blankets between the mattress and springs of your bed. Your blankets are then out of the way and easily accessible.

6

LAUNDERING

WASH BEFORE YOU WEAR

When new clothing has a chemical finish or a dye that is particularly disagreeable to a sensitive nose, treat it before you wear it. First, make sure it's washable and colorfast (see COLORFAST TESTING below). Then presoak the garment for a few hours in the sink or basin with ½ cup baking soda to 1 gallon water. After soaking, throw it in the washing machine and add ½ cup white vinegar to the rinse cycle.

BLEACH ALTERNATIVES

Use ¼ to ½ cup lemon juice, ¼ cup white vinegar or 3 tablespoons hydrogen peroxide in your wash instead of bleach.

For lingerie or other delicate fabrics whose washing instructions suggest a gentle bleach, use 1 part hydrogen peroxide to 8 parts water. Soak the garment in the mixture for about fifteen minutes, then rinse thoroughly.

WHEN WHITES GET DINGY

Cut ½ lemon into slices and put them in a basin of boiling hot water. Soak the once-white socks, handkerchiefs, and underwear for at least a half hour. Wash as usual.

As you machine-wash graying whites, dissolve one tablespoon borax in a pint of hot water and pour it into the last rinse cycle.

Folk Belief: New Clothing

When you wear a new garment for the first time,

have a friend pinch you for luck.

An old custom is to wish the wearer of the new garment "health to

wear it, strength to tear it, and money to buy another."

WASHING LONG-SLEEVED GARMENTS

To prevent shirt and blouse sleeves from tangling in the washing machine, button the cuffs to the front of the garment.

DRAWSTRINGS

At the end of each drawstring simply make a knot or sew a button that's big enough to prevent the ends from disappearing into the garment holes.

LINT

• **To Remove:** This may sound silly, but Silly Putty can remove lint from clothes. Use it as you would a blotter.

   Wind masking or transparent tape—sticky side out—around the cardboard cylinder from a paper-towel roll and you'll have a do-it-yourself lint remover. Just roll it over the areas with lint.

• **To Keep Dark Fabrics and Corduroy Lint-Free:** Add ½ cup white vinegar to the last rinse cycle.

WASHER/DRYER TIP

Put a piece of brown paper, linoleum, or carpet on the floor in between the washer and dryer, so that when a sock or other item of clothing slips down you can pull out the strip and easily retrieve the dropped whatever.

WASH THE WASHING MACHINE

At least once a year, fill the washing machine with hot water, add one quart white vinegar, and put it through the wash and rinse cycles.

CLOTHESLINE

If you still use a clothesline, good for you! In cold weather, pour ¼ cup salt into the last rinse cycle to prevent wet clothes from freezing on the clothesline. The salt may also brighten your wash.

If you didn't add salt during the last rinse cycle, sponge down the clothesline with white vinegar to avoid clothes-to-clothesline freeze.

COLORFAST TESTING

If you're not sure whether or not a garment is colorfast, rub an inside seam of the garment with a clean, white, wet washcloth. If the color doesn't come off on the cloth, the garment is colorfast. If the color is on the cloth, the garment is not colorfast, and if you throw it in a wash with other clothes, everything will turn that color. Read on for ways to make clothes colorfast.

SET COLORS ON NONCOLORFAST CLOTHES

If the label of a garment doesn't say "Colorfast," chances are the color will run. The following treatment should set the color so that it will not run or fade: Dissolve 1 teaspoon Epsom salts in 1 gallon water and soak the colorful garment in it overnight. Next morning, rinse thoroughly with vinegar water—¼ cup vinegar in 1 gallon of water. Should you throw this treated garment in with your wash? Do the inside seam test (above) again and then use your discretion, but please don't hold us responsible.

RING AROUND THE COLLAR

• **To Clean:** Mix equal parts water and shampoo (use the nondesigner kind in which the first ingredient is *water,* not *oil*), then rub it on the ring around the collar and let it sink in for thirty minutes. Thoroughly wash and rinse with warm water.

• **To Prevent:** Before putting on the collared shirt or blouse, clean the oil off your neck with witch hazel or rubbing alcohol.

WRINKLE-FREE MACHINE DRYING

• **Don't Overcrowd the Dryer:** The more crowded the dryer, the more the clothes will wrinkle. If you have a big wash load, divide it into two dryers or two drying sessions, giving the clothes more room to straighten out and dry.

• **Wash-and-Wear:** After laundering a wash-and-wear garment, rinse it in cool water for minimal wrinkling.

When a wash-and-wear garment is wrinkled, place it in the dryer with a damp towel for about ten minutes. Or just iron it!

FLUFFING UP YOUR DOWN

After washing a down-filled jacket, vest, coat, or comforter, toss it in the dryer along with three or four tennis balls or a pair of clean sneakers. The balls or sneakers will reduce static cling while fluffing up the item.

WOOLENS, SWEATERS

• **To Reshape:** When the turtleneck, cuffs, and waist of a sweater get that stretched-out look, dip them into a sink of hot water, pat them down with a towel until they stop dripping, and then dry them with a blow dryer set on *hot.* That should shrink them back into shape.

• **To Remove Pills:** To remove the little pill-like balls from a sweater, brush them. Of all the brushes we tried, a wig brush with tiny plastic balls at the end of the bristles worked best. It also helped to keep changing direction when brushing the sweater. Brush up, brush sideways, brush down—but always brush gently. And remember, this depilling process makes the sweater better, but not like new.

• **To Prevent Pilling:** Turn the garment inside out when you wash it.

• **To Prevent Itchiness:** Wash woolens in warm water and add one or two tablespoons glycerine (available at drugstores) to prevent the clothes from being too scratchy when you wear them.

JEANS

• **To Soften New Jeans:** Run them through the washing machine with detergent and ½ cup salt.

• **To Prevent Streaking:** Wash them inside out.

• **To Prevent Fading:** Soak them for an hour in a mixture of two tablespoons salt and one gallon cold water. Then, turn them inside out and throw them in the washing machine, which is set for cold water.

• **To Perk Up Faded Jeans:** Wash them a few times with a pair of new jeans. The dye from the new pair will be absorbed by the faded pair. Then again, if you have a new pair, you probably won't care about the faded pair.

Folk Belief: Inside-out Clothing

If you unknowingly wear an article of clothing inside out,

it will be a lucky day.

SILK

• **To Wash Washable Silk:** Use hair shampoo whose first ingredient is *water,* not oil, and contains *protein* to feed the protein in the silk. Be gentle with silk. Don't twist or wring it. Let it drip-dry away from direct sunlight.

PET HAIR

• **To Remove:** Moisten a sponge with warm water and lightly run it over the hairy clothes. Or use transparent-tape strips to blot off the hair.

WASHING DELICATE ITEMS

• **In the Washing Machine:** If you want to machine-wash your delicates, put them in a pillowcase, tie it closed, then throw it in the machine.
• **By Hand:** Put your delicates into a big jar with water and one or two teaspoons dishwashing liquid. Then shake the jar for a couple of minutes, rinse, and air-dry the items.

PREPPING CLOTHES FOR THE MACHINE

• **General Rule:** Before machine-washing and drying clothes, turn them inside out to minimize the wear on them, especially on the edges and creases. You'll have less fading and pilling of knits,

Folk Belief: Lingerie

If you're single and a recently married woman gives you lingerie,

you can expect to march down the aisle within the year.

permanent-press, and quilted fabrics, as well as less lint on corduroy garments.

DETERGENT

• **For Best Results:** Follow the manufacturer's recommendation on the label for the amount of detergent to use. *More* is not better. In fact, *more* can prevent clothes from getting their cleanest and from being thoroughly rinsed.

• **Fighting Too Many Suds:** If you mismeasured and want to get rid of the excess suds that are preventing the washer from agitating freely, sprinkle a little salt into the machine. Or, if you're sure it's a colorfast load, pour two tablespoons of vinegar into the wash water.

• **Using the Right Detergent:** It is not a good idea to substitute dishwashing liquid for laundry detergent. The amount of liquid you would need to get clothes clean would create an *I Love Lucy* scene, with suds everywhere and you *waaaaaahing.* The overflowing mess would be beyond a salt cure.

FABRIC SOFTENERS

• **Warning:** Fabric-softener sheets can stain polyester garments in the dryer, and fabric-softener liquid poured directly on clothes can also stain them. Follow directions on the package and *proceed cautiously.*

• **Asthmatics Beware:** Fabric softeners used on bedding, as well as on clothing, have been known to cause allergic reactions. If you are sensitive in this way, be forewarned.

• **Economical Softening:** Instead of using expensive tear-off fabric-softener *sheets,* buy the liquid, dilute it with water, dab some on a washcloth and throw it into the dryer with the rest of your wash.

• **Substitute Softener:** One-quarter cup white vinegar added to the last rinse cycle is a good fabric softener—and then some. It also brightens colors and helps do away with mold and fungus, such as that from socks worn by an athlete's foot sufferer. But remember, while your wash will *not* come out smelling like vinegar, it will not have that springlike fabric-softener smell either.

HARD WATER

• **A Test:** If you wonder why your clothes aren't getting clean, it may be because you have *hard water*. Here's a simple way to test for hard water: take a quart jar of warm water and add ½ teaspoon detergent. Close the jar and vigorously shake it. If it doesn't suds up, or if the few suds that are there disappear faster than they should, you have hard water. Now what? Read on. . . .

• **Hard-Water Remedy:** Combine ½ pound washing soda with ¼ pound borax in 1 gallon of water. Store the solution in a couple of plastic bottles. Each time you do a wash, add a cup of it to the wash water to soften it.

CLOTHES HAMPER

• **Keep It Deodorized:** If you don't do a wash every day and odor-iferous clothes—such as teenagers' socks—pile up, sprinkle baking soda daily on the clothes in the hamper. It will not only keep the hamper from smelling like dirty clothes, but also help the clothes smell fresher and feel softer when you eventually do the wash.

IRONING

• **To Prevent Mineral Deposits:** Fill your iron with distilled water instead of tap water.

• **If Ironing Has to Wait:** Put damp clothes in a plastic bag and store in the freezer. You'll prevent mildew, and you won't have to redampen the clothes. You may, however, have to wait until they thaw out a bit.

• **For More Efficient Ironing:** Place a long, smooth sheet of aluminum foil under the ironing-board cover. It will reflect and hold the heat and help cut down on ironing time.

• **To Prep Clothes for Ironing:** Dampen with warm water rather than cold, and the ironing will go quicker and come out better.

• **Impromptu Sleeve Board:** A rolled-up towel slid into the sleeve will allow the sleeve to be ironed without creating a crease.

• **To Prevent Puckering:** Iron collars, cuffs, and hems on the wrong side first.

• **To Get Rid of a Hemline Crease:** After lengthening a skirt by letting down the hem, sponge the crease of the original hemline with white vinegar on the wrong side of the fabric. Place a moist cloth over the dampened crease, then zap it with a hot iron.

• **To Prevent Scorching:** If you have an especially scorchable garment, carefully iron it between two pieces of aluminum foil.

• **To Prevent a Shine:** Linens, dark cottons, rayons, and silks should all be ironed on the wrong side. For delicate clothing, cover the fabric with a sheet of tissue paper and use a cooler-than-usual iron.

• **Ironing Velvet and Velveteen:** Never put the iron directly on the fabric. Dampen a white cloth (*pressing cloths* manufactured for this purpose are inexpensive and sold at most hardware stores and supermarkets) and place it on the garment. Then gently iron the cloth as it sizzles.

• **Don't Sweep the Floor with Clean Clothes:** Keep spring-type clothespins handy so that while you're ironing a blouse or shirt you can clamp the sleeves together instead of having them dangle on the floor. Clothespin clamping works for scarves and full skirts, too.

• **Ironing Pleats:** Use bobby pins or spring-type clothespins on the hem to hold pleats in place. Once you've ironed the body of a pleated skirt, remove the bobby pins or clothespins and complete the job by ironing the hem.

• **Don't Iron Dirty Clothes:** The heat of the iron may set the dirt stains forever.

• **Minimize Pants Pressing:** After washing pants, hang them to dry by the ends of the legs rather than by the waist. The heavier wet portion of the pants will pull out the wrinkles as it dries, and you may not need to iron them at all.

PANTYHOSE

• **Longevity:** Before you wear new pantyhose, dip them in water, wring them out, enclose them in a plastic bag and freeze them solid. When you take them out of the freezer, let them thaw and dry completely. Then wear them well.

Add a drop of liquid fabric softener to the water when you rinse pantyhose. The softener will lubricate the fibers, giving them a longer life.

• **To Increase Elasticity:** Add two tablespoons white vinegar to the rinse water to help pantyhose keep their elasticity.

• **To Wash:** Use an old pantyhose leg to hold pairs of good pantyhose when washing them in a washing machine. Be sure to knot the pantyhose leg closed at the top so the stockings won't fall out in the washing machine.

• **Buy Two, Get an Extra One Free:** When you buy two of the exact same kind of pantyhose, you can have a wearability of three pairs. Huh? When a leg of the first pair gets a run, do not throw it away. Wait until the second pair gets a run in one leg. You then cut off and discard the legs with runs, leaving you with two panty parts, each with one leg. Put them both on and—*voilà!*—a run-free pair of pantyhose.

TAKING CLOTHES OUT OF MOTHBALLS

• **To Eliminate Odor:** When clothes reek of mothballs, air them out for several hours, then put them in a warm clothes dryer for about fifteen minutes. Check the information on FABRIC SOFTENERS (above), and decide whether or not to throw in a scented fabric-softener sheet.

Folk Belief: Stockings, Pantyhose, Tights, and Socks

If the legs of stockings, pantyhose, tights, leggings, or socks intertwine

on a clothesline, or in a dryer, the owner of the garment is assured

of joy and happiness.

CURTAINS

• **To Freshen Dacron and Nylon Curtains:** Wash and rinse as usual. Then, in a sink or basin, mix one cup Epsom salts in a gallon of water. Soak the curtains—one panel at a time—for a few minutes, and hang them up. They should dry wrinkle-free, looking like new.

• **For Wrinkle-Free Sheer Curtains:** Machine-wash your washable sheer curtains as usual. Prepare a packet of unflavored gelatin in a cup of just-boiled water. Then, for the final rinse cycle, pour in the gelatin, and you can forget about setting up the iron.

• **To Hang Curtains Safely:** To easily glide curtains on a curtain rod, put a thimble or a finger from a discarded old glove on the end of the rod. If you're using a flat rod, stick a butter knife into the rod's slit end. That way, when you slide the curtain over the thimble, glove finger, or butter knife, it will go on faster—without tearing or snagging.

PLASTICS: TABLECLOTHS, MATS, AND CURTAINS
(See Chapter 8, "Bathroom," for PLASTIC SHOWER CURTAIN.)

• **To Get the Smell Out:** Most plastic items will lose that unpleasant smell of plastic soon after they're unwrapped and exposed to the air. On the rare occasion when the smell hangs on, soak the item in a sink or basin with ½ cup baking soda. If you also want to soften the item and make it more pliable, add ½ cup white vinegar. Leave it soaking for a few hours, then rinse and air-dry.

• **To Machine-Wash:** If the tablecloth, mats, or curtains are machine-washable, wash them along with a couple of bath towels. The towels will act as buffers while scrubbing the plastic clean. If you also add one cup vinegar during the last rinse cycle, the plastic items will come out soft and pliable. Then put them in the dryer *with* the towels, but for only a few minutes, and they will come out fairly

Folk Belief: Towel Dropping

Accidentally dropping a towel is a sign that someone will show up

at your door unexpectedly. If you're not in the mood for company,

simply and carefully walk over the towel backward,

and the visitor might decide to drop in on someone else.

wrinkle-free. Be sure to check the dryer frequently, though, because you don't want to overdo the drying time for anything plastic.

STAINS

PLEASE READ THIS FIRST

The stain-removal suggestions given below have all worked for the people who have passed them along, or we would not have included them in the book. Even so, we urge you to test any stain remover on an area of your garment that is not visible. That way, if it is not good for the fabric, you will not further spoil the garment.

BABY FORMULA

Meat tenderizer (unseasoned) has an enzyme that breaks down the protein in milk and baby formula. Rub a paste of tenderizer and water on stains and leave them for about an hour. Then wash the garment as usual.

If you've already tried to wash and bleach out a baby-formula stain with no luck, douse it with lemon juice and put it in the sun for thirty minutes. If the stain doesn't disappear completely, repeat the procedure one more time.

BALLPOINT PEN (see INK below.)

BEER

Beer will wash out when you wash the stained garment in warm soapsuds.

BLOOD

As soon as you discover the bloodstain, rinse it with *cold* water. (*Hot* water can set the stain.) Then make a paste of unseasoned meat tenderizer with cold water and put it on the stain. Half an hour later, rinse off the paste and wash the garment as usual.

Cover a bloodstain with a few drops of hydrogen peroxide. Don't get scared when you see it fizz. That's what happens before the stain disappears. Remember, test first!

If you've already washed a bloodstain and it hasn't come out, soak the stain in a mixture of two tablespoons salt and one cup water. Leave it for fifteen minutes, then wash as usual.

CANDLE WAX

(Use the CHEWING GUM remedy below.)

CHEWING GUM

Place the garment in a plastic bag and in the freezer for at least an hour. By then, the gum will have frozen and you can crumble it off.

COFFEE OR TEA

• **In a Restaurant:** Wet a clean white napkin with seltzer or club soda and wipe the stained area. If the stain needs more work, rub salt on the spot and leave it on for about ten minutes, then wipe it off. Wash the garment as soon as you get home.

• **At Home:** Spread the stained area over a pot (or bowl) and secure it in place with a rubber band. Put the pot in the kitchen sink, then slowly and carefully pour just-boiled water—from a height of at least twenty inches—through the stained fabric. Be very careful.

• **White Linen, Cotton, or Lace:** Spread out the stained cloth in the sink or bathtub (depending on how much room is needed) and dampen the stained area with warm water. Dissolve two denture-cleaning tablets in ½ cup warm water. While it's still fizzing, pour the denture cleaner on the stain, and leave it for about a half hour. Then wash as usual. Remember, this is for *white* items only.

FRUIT (INCLUDING BERRIES) AND FRUIT JUICE

• **Clothes:** Sponge the stain with cold water as soon as possible. Then, if it's practical for you and safe for the fabric, spread the stained area over a pot (or bowl) and secure it in place with a rubber band. Put the pot in the kitchen sink, then slowly and carefully pour just-boiled water—from a height of at least twenty inches—through the stained fabric. If the stain isn't completely out, massage laundry detergent or hydrogen peroxide into the area, then rinse.

• **Table Linen:** As soon as possible, cover the fruit stain with powdered starch and leave it on for three to four hours. Then wash as usual.

GRASS

• **Clothes:** Brush white non-gel toothpaste into grass stains, then rinse and wash as usual.

• **Jeans:** Dab rubbing alcohol on grass stains, and after about ten minutes, throw the jeans in with the rest of the wash.

• **White-Leather Shoes:** Massage the grass stains with molasses and leave it on overnight. Next morning, wash the molasses off the shoes with soap and water and the grass stains should be gone.

• **Suede Shoes:** Rub the stain with a sponge that's been dipped in glycerine (available at drugstores).

GRAVY

Soak the stain in cold water long enough to dissolve the gravy's starch, then wash as usual.

GREASE

Rub cornstarch or talcum powder into a stain and let it sit for at least fifteen minutes, allowing time for the powder to absorb the grease, then brush off the powder. If the powder reduced the amount of grease but didn't get rid of it completely, repeat the process.
• **Work Clothes:** Loosen the grease and grime by pouring a bottle of cola in the washing machine along with the detergent.

INK

Tomato juice or slices of raw tomato on stains should soak up the ink. Then wash as usual.

Sponge the stains with milk until the stain is gone.

KETCHUP, TOMATO SAUCE, CHILI SAUCE, BARBECUE SAUCE

Wet the stain with cold water, and sponge it with glycerine. Let it sit for one-half hour, then wash in warm soapsuds. If the stain isn't completely gone, sponge it with hydrogen peroxide, then rinse in cold water.

LIPSTICK

• **Clothes:** Blot off as much as possible with white bread, then wash as usual.

Brush with a white non-gel toothpaste, then wash as usual.
• **Napkins:** *Throughout this process, keep a dry paper towel under the fabric's stain.* Dampen a cloth with rubbing alcohol and use it to press down on the stain over and over to blot it up. Then wash as usual.

MAKEUP

Sprinkle baking soda on the makeup smudge, then with a wet toothbrush brush the area until the stain is gone.

Try rubbing the smudge off with white bread or stale rye bread.

PERSPIRATION

• **Cotton or Polyester Knits:** Add enough water to a scoop of baking soda to make a paste. Apply the paste to the perspiration stains and leave it on for fifteen minutes before throwing it in the machine with the rest of the wash. It should come out smell-free as well as stain-free.

• **Woolens:** Soak the garment for thirty minutes in a mixture of ¼ cup salt and 1 quart cold water. Then wash as usual.

If, after a garment has been washed, it still has perspiration odor, wet the area with a solution of one teaspoon white vinegar and one cup water. Let it stand for one hour, then wash as usual.

RUST

Boil the (washable) rust-stained garment in a mixture of two tablespoons cream of tartar and one quart water for about ten minutes. Then rinse and hang it up to dry—but not on a metal hanger. That may be how you got the rust stains in the first place.

Drench the rust spots with lemon juice and hang the garment in the sun. Then wash as usual.

SCORCH MARKS

Dampen a cloth with white vinegar and place it over the scorched patch, then apply a warm iron. Proceed cautiously so that you don't make it worse.

• **Light Scorch Marks on Linen:** Take a wedge of yellow onion, rub it on the scorch marks, then soak the linen garment in cold water before laundering.

SKUNK SMELL

To get out the stench from a skunk spray, presoak clothes for a few hours in the sink or a basin with ½ cup baking soda to 1 gallon water. After soaking, throw the clothes in the washing machine and add ½ cup white vinegar to the rinse cycle.

SHOES AND BOOTS

• **For Longevity:** It has been tested and proven that three pairs of shoes worn alternately will last as long as four pairs of shoes that weren't rotated. It makes sense, considering that the average pair of feet give off more than ½ pint of sweat every day. Is this more than you wanted to know? What you *really* need to know is that you should let the shoes you're wearing today air out for a full twenty-four hours before wearing them again.

• **Scuff Marks:** Wipe scuff marks off leather shoes with a paste of baking soda and water or with an art-gum eraser (available wherever you buy art supplies).

• **White Shoes:** If neither of the above works, cover the scuff marks with liquid typewriter correction fluid, then, if necessary, polish the shoes. If you don't have correction fluid, prep the shoes for white polish by rubbing them with a piece of raw potato. The potato will help the polish go on smoothly and cover the scuff marks.

• **Black Shoes:** Cover up the scrapes with India ink or Magic Marker.

Folk Belief: Shoes

Oh, happy day when you start off by putting the right shoe

on first, then the left one.

• **Substitute Shoe Polish:** Put a light coat of floor wax or furniture polish on your shoes, wipe dry, and then buff them with a soft cloth.

• **To Waterproof Shoes:** Polish them, then follow up with a light coat of floor wax. While you shouldn't go wading in water, this treatment will make your shoes somewhat waterproof.

• **To Dry Wet Shoes:** Stuff newspaper pages in wet shoes or spill uncooked oatmeal in them, then let them dry naturally. Keep them out of the sun and away from direct heat. When they're thoroughly dry, rub them with a piece of raw potato, then polish.

• **To Dry Boots While Camping Out:** This remedy is good only if the wet boots do *not* have a synthetic lining. Use the campfire to heat up several clean pebbles. Pour them into the boots and shake them around until the pebbles are cool. The moisture will dry out as the heat is absorbed by the boot.

• **Salt Stains, Wet Rings:** Wipe salt stains off shoes or boots with a mixture of equal parts of white vinegar and water.

If you're out of vinegar, wipe off the salt stains with a piece of potato.

• **Patent Leather:** Gently massage patent shoes with a soft cloth that's dampened with almond oil or baby oil. Then buff with a soft dry cloth.

• **Suede Shoes:** Remove grease stains by wiping with a cloth dampened with white vinegar.

Folk Belief: Lender's Boots

When you want to borrow money, look down at people's pants and boots.

The person who has money to lend will have one pant leg in his boot

and one pant leg out of his boot.

• **To Deodorize Shoes:** Scatter baking soda or salt inside smelly shoes or sneakers. Give it twenty-four hours to fully absorb the odor. Shake the shoes out, and they're ready to wear again.

• **To Ease a Tight Spot:** Rubbing alcohol rubbed on a tight spot on the inside of the shoe will ease the leather temporarily until you can get the shoe permanently stretched.

• **To Stretch Leather Shoes:** For each shoe, use either a heavy-weight plastic kitchen bag, or two bags, putting one inside the other, and put them in each shoe. Pour water into the bags, filling your shoes, and be sure to close the bags securely so that the water doesn't seep out and wet the shoes. To help prevent the outside of the shoes from getting wet, put each one in a plastic bag. Then place the shoes in the freezer for twenty-four hours. As water freezes, it expands, and as it expands in the shoes, the shoes will stretch. Since this helpful hint is part of the title of our book, we want to make it clear. So let's review this:

> • plastic bag goes in shoe
> • water goes in plastic bag
> • shoe goes in another plastic bag
> • it all goes in the freezer

A day later, when you take the shoes out of the freezer, you may need to give it some thaw time until you're able to take the ice-filled plastic bags out of your shoes. *Now* if you have cold feet, at least you have a good reason.

• **Gold or Silver Shoes:** Brush away scuff marks on gold or silver shoes with white non-gel toothpaste on a toothbrush.

SHOELACES

• **To Keep Them Tied:** Dampen your shoelaces before tying them, and they will stay tied.

• **Replacing the Shoelace Tip:** When you have lost the plastic tip of the shoelace (also known in Trivial Pursuit circles as the *aglet*), create a new aglet by dipping the end of the shoelace in colorless nail polish and shaping it into a point with a pair of tweezers. Be sure to let it dry thoroughly. It takes a while.

Wrap transparent tape tightly around the frayed ends of shoelaces to form new aglets.

LEATHER LUGGAGE

• **To Remove Black Scuff Marks:** Rub on lemon extract, then wipe it off. (Also see SCUFF MARKS under SHOES AND BOOTS above.)
• **To Brighten Leather:** With a cloth dampened with egg white, give the leather a light coat. After a few minutes, wipe off and buff with a soft cloth.

LEATHER GLOVES

• **To Erase Stains:** Rub the stains with an art-gum eraser (available where art supplies are sold).
• **To Remove an Oil Stain:** Cover the stain with cornstarch. Leave it overnight, then brush it off.
• **To Clean White Kid Gloves:** Massage flour into the dirt, then brush it off.

Folk Belief: Dropped Gloves

Next time you drop a glove, let someone else pick it up and hand it to you.

In addition to the pleasant surprise that someone actually picked up

the glove for you, you can expect another pleasant surprise

in the very near future.

FELT HATS

• **To Clean:** In a jar, combine one cup cornmeal with one cup salt. Shake it until the cornmeal and salt are thoroughly mixed. Brush the hat with a whisk broom or a soft hairbrush. Next, by hand, massage the cornmeal-salt mixture into the hat, leave it for about five minutes, then brush the hat again.

• **To Zap the Nap:** If the felt's fuzzy surface needs to be spruced up, carefully—very carefully—hold it over the steaming spout of a teapot, far enough away so that you don't scald yourself. Once the steam has had a go at the entire chapeau, let it air-dry for a few minutes, then brush it, and it should look like new.

7

SEWING

PINS AND NEEDLES

• **For Easy Pickup:** Glue a magnet to the end of a yardstick and use it to pick up those pins and needles that find their way to the floor.

• **For Easy Gliding:** If you have trouble pushing a pin or needle through fabric, and your hair is on the oily side, *very carefully* rub the needle or pin through your hair, then try again.

An even better and safer idea is to use a thick candle or a big bar of soap as a pincushion. It will hold your pins and needles and wax them at the same time.

• **To Sharpen:** Buff the tips of pins or needles with an emery board.

Put a couple of steel-wool pads in a little drawstring pouch and use that as a pincushion. The steel wool will sharpen your pins and needles each time you stick one in or take it out.

Folk Belief: Pins

See a pin, pick it up, and all the day you'll have good luck.

• **Easy Needle Threading:** A little spritz of hair spray on the end of the thread will make it stiff and easier to put through the eye of the needle.

Dip the tip of the thread in colorless nail polish and it will dry stiff enough to thread.

SEWING-MACHINE NEEDLE

• **To Sharpen:** Sew through a piece of fine sandpaper with a sewing-machine needle.

THREAD

• **To Prevent Tangles:** To keep thread from knotting and tangling as you sew with it, run the piece of thread through a sheet of fabric softener right before using it, and it should behave.

To keep thread neat and untangled, place a rubber band around each spool, keeping each thread end under wraps.

WORKING WITH A PATTERN

• **To Get an Accurate Pattern Size:** A creased pattern piece can alter the size of a garment. Always iron pattern sections before laying them on the fabric to be cut.

Folk Belief: Good-Luck Thread

If, while you're sewing, the thread wraps itself around the needle,

you can expect good health and good luck.

Folk Belief: Mending While Wearing

If clothing is being mended while being worn, it is believed in certain

(sewing) circles that the wearer must chew on a piece of thread during the

process to prevent the sewing up of his or her common sense.

SEWING A HEM

• **Measuring and Marking the Hem:** If you use a ruler to measure the number of inches to turn up a hem, or a yardstick to mark the inches from the floor to the hemline, put a rubber band around that exact line on the ruler or yardstick. It will make the marking process easier and go a lot faster.

• **Alternatives to Pinning:** Tired of sticking yourself while pinning a new hem? Try using spring-type clothespins or paper clips to keep the hem in place while you sew it.

• **To Hem Jeans:** It's no fun to sew denim. It's also not necessary, if all you need is a hem on your jeans. Turn up the hem, iron, and hold it in place with duct tape. There's the standard silver duct tape—and now a whole array of other colors. The taped hem should last through many washings.

• **Temporary Hems:** Have you ever caught your heel in your hem and brought down that section of it? If you need to make a temporary repair, use double-sided tape to patch up a fallen hem or a hanging lining. Second best is duct tape. If worse comes to worst, just safety-pin or staple the hem up.

HEMLINE CREASES

• **To Iron Out the Crease:** As hemlines change, hemline crease marks increase. Get rid of a telltale hemline by sponging white vine-

Folk Belief: Hemline Happiness

When you're dressing for something special, check out your hemline in a mirror. If any part of it is turned up, you will be surrounded by good luck.

gar on the wrong side of the fabric. Place a moist cloth over the crease then zap it with a hot iron. No crease. No shine. No fooling.

BASTING

• **No Rethreading:** Instead of cutting off a piece of thread for basting and then having to rethread, just work off the spool.

WAISTBAND EXTENDER

• **To Add Inches to the Waistline:** (Warning: This is going to sound more complicated than it actually is.) Using one-inch-wide elastic, cut a length that is the number of inches you need to extend the waistband. On one end of the piece of elastic sew a button that's comparable in size to the one that is already on the waistband. On the other end of the piece of elastic cut a buttonhole-size slit. The waistband button goes through that slit, while the button on the elastic goes in the original buttonhole. Got it? Good!

POCKETS

• **To Protect a Pocket:** The second it feels as though a pocket is wearing out, reinforce it with iron-on tape.

PATCHES

• **Prepatch Preparation:** Be sure to launder fabric before it is used as a patch. You wouldn't want a patch to shrink after it has been sewn on a garment.

• **To Patch a Patch:** A little Elmer's-type glue will hold a patch in place while you sew it on. The glue will disappear next time the garment is washed.

When you're applying an iron-on patch to cover a hole in a garment, place a piece of aluminum foil under the hole to prevent the patch from sticking to the ironing-board cover.

• **To Remove an Iron-on Patch:** Zap an iron-on patch with a hot iron and it should peel right off.

• **To Patch Jeans:** Time was when people added longer life to their children's jeans by ironing on knee patches on the *inside* of the jeans. Now torn knees in jeans are the style. Who knows, by the time you read this, we may be back to reinforced knees—this time on the *outside* of jeans.

Speaking of jeans . . . You may want to wear an old pair while working around the house or garden, or while roller-blading. Sew knee patches on those old jeans, and leave a few inches open on top. Insert a pair of shoulder pads that have been hanging around, kitchen sponges, or any kind of foam rubber that will protect your knees.

BUTTONS

• **Button Storage:** Use a clear glass jar for buttons so that you can see at a glance if what you need is there.

To avoid hunting expeditions, organize your loose buttons according to your needs. Use dental floss to string same-size or same-color buttons together. String together those extra-in-case-one-falls-off buttons that come with new clothes. Sets of buttons can also be put on large safety pins.

• **To Sew on Buttons:** Use a big-eyed needle and double the thread, then thread the needle. You will be sewing with four strands, so you'll only need a couple of stitches to secure the button.

To make sure buttons won't fall off, especially on children's clothes, use dental floss or nylon fishing line to sew them on. If the white floss is too noticeable, cover the floss with thread that matches the garment.

Buttons will stay on longer if you dab a little glue or colorless nail polish on the thread in the center of each button, both front and back.

For four-hole buttons, proceed as though you're sewing on two two-hole buttons, and the button will hold better. Think about it.

• **To Remove Buttons:** To make sure you don't cut or tear the fabric when removing a button, let a comb run interference: Slide the comb under the button and then, with a razor blade or knife between the fabric and the comb, cut the thread.

ZIPPERS

• **To Replace a Lost Pull Tab:** Use a small paper clip. Paper clips come not only in the standard silver, but now are also in gold and just about every other color.

Folk Belief: Buttons for a New Year

The first person you meet on New Year's Day can give you a glimpse of your

future. All you have to do is count the number of buttons he or she has on.

One button and you're in for a lucky year; two buttons and happiness is

yours; three means a new vehicle for you; four and you can plan on

an alternative mode of transportation; five will get you a new wardrobe;

six, just the accessories; seven, a new dog; eight, a new cat; nine,

an unexpected letter; ten, pleasure; eleven, extreme joy;

twelve buttons, and you will soon discover a treasure.

8

BATHROOM

AIR FRESHENER

Before company comes, leave out a small bowl of vinegar or lemon juice or an open box of baking soda to absorb bathroom odors.

When company comes, light scented candles in the bathroom. (Be sure the candles are in secure holders and safe places.) They help eliminate odors, call less attention to the room's disarray, and make your guests look great.

TOILET BOWL

• **To Clean and Deodorize:** When in doubt, get the baking soda out. Some housekeepers sprinkle baking soda into the bowl, scrub with a toilet brush, wait a few minutes, then flush. Others sprinkle the soda and follow it with some white vinegar, let it sit for five minutes, then scour with a brush and flush. The vinegar is a good deodorizer and disinfectant. In fact, the vinegar alone can be used to clean the bowl.

Once a month, before bedtime, you might want to scatter one-half box of baking soda in the toilet tank and let it stand overnight. Then flush in the morning for a clean tank and bowl.

Pour a cola soft drink in the bowl and let it soak awhile, then flush and notice how it brightens the bowl.

Tang may be the drink of astronauts, but to us it's an effective swell-smelling toilet-bowl stain remover. No kidding! Sprinkle about

⅓ cup Tang powder in the bowl. Leave it there for a couple of hours, then flush.

For tough toilet stains, empty a few vitamin C capsules in the bowl, or mash the tablets and sprinkle the powder in the bowl. Let it stay overnight. In the morning, scrub with a brush, then flush.

Just when you thought you had heard it all, there's one more. Drop a couple of denture-cleaning tablets in the bowl. Once the fizzing stops, scrub the stains and flush. You can also clean the tank by dropping in a denture tablet or two.

MOISTURE, MOLD, AND MILDEW

• **To Absorb Moisture:** If you like taking hot showers and you're troubled by the moisture that can cause mold and mildew, keep a few charcoal briquettes in the bathroom to help absorb some of that moisture.

• **To Prevent a Steamy Bathroom:** Before you relax in that wonderful warm bath, layer the tub with an inch of cold water, then run the hot water on top of it. It should prevent the room from steaming up.

• **To Remove Mold and Mildew:** Take a cloth dampened with lemon juice and sprinkle salt on it, then use it to clean off a mildewed area.

• **To Prevent Mildew:** Planning a long trip? No need to come home to a mildewed bathroom if you leave an open bag of (moisture-absorbing) kitty litter in your bathtub.

MIRROR

• **To Prevent Steaming:** Before you take a hot shower, moisten a cloth with glycerine and spread a thin layer across the mirror. Or clean the mirror with shaving cream to keep it steam-free.

• **To Remove Hair Spray:** A cloth dampened with rubbing alcohol will clean off hair spray.

CHROME FAUCETS

• **To Clean and Shine:** White vinegar on a cloth or sponge will clean water spots and soap scum off chrome bathroom fixtures. Dry and buff with a soft cloth.

Folk Belief: Broken Mirror Antidote

Of course you all know about breaking a mirror and the seven years

of bad luck that supposedly follow, but do you also know the ways to

counteract the effect? Here are three:

As soon as you realize what you've done, turn around three times

counterclockwise. (Be careful not to step on the broken pieces of

mirror. Now that's bad luck.)

When it's dark out, light seven white candles. At midnight, take a

deep breath and blow them all out.

Take a piece of the broken mirror to a cemetery and tap a gravestone

with it. Any one of the above should do it—or rather undo it.

Rubbing alcohol will also clean and shine bathroom chrome.
• **To Shine:** You're going to need your sunglasses after you use fabric-softener sheets to shine the chrome fixtures.
• **To Remove Hard-Water Buildup** (see SHOWERHEAD at the end of this chapter).

SOAP

• **For Longevity:** Keep a bar of soap unwrapped for about a month before you use it. This aging process will give the soap longer life.

SOAP DISH

• **To Prevent Soap-Dish Mess:** Find an appropriate waterproof object, like the round plastic core that's discarded once a roll of transparent tape is used up, and rest it on the soap dish with the soap on top of it. It will prevent the wet soap from mushing up and from scumming up the soap dish.

Line a soap dish with a piece of sponge and let the sponge soak up the soap's water and film.

Just use a sponge as a soap dish.

TILE AND TILE GROUT

• **To Clean:** Sponge white vinegar on the tile and grout, then scrub the grout with an old toothbrush and rinse clean.

• **To Whiten Grout:** If old, yellowed grout just won't whiten by cleaning, try white liquid shoe polish on it. Or wet a nail-whitener pencil and go over the grout with it.

BATHTUB MAT

• **To Clean:** A rubber or vinyl bathtub mat will look like new after you put it in the washing machine with your towels. The terry-cloth towels will scour the mat clean.

NONSLIP BATHTUB APPLIQUÉS

• **To Remove:** Place aluminum foil on the nonslip appliqués in the tub and zap 'em with a blow dryer. The heat should help unstick each appliqué, making it possible to peel them off.

Drench a cloth or sponge in hot vinegar and place it on the appliqué. When the vinegar cools to room temperature you should then be able to lift off the appliqué.

Dip a utility knife or a straight-edge razor blade in dishwashing detergent, and carefully scrape off the appliqué.

• **To Remove Adhesive:** If, after using any of the above, some adhesive gunk is left on the tub, nail-polish remover should finish the job.

BATHTUB

• **General Cleaning Rule:** Dirt comes off more easily when you clean right after someone has bathed or showered because the bathroom is warm and humid.

• **General Cleaning Tip:** Protect your knees while cleaning the tub by kneeling on two sponges or a couple of shoulder pads.

• **To Clean:** Wet a washcloth with vinegar, sprinkle baking soda around the tub, then scrub and rinse. No harmful chemicals. No drain-clogging cleansers. No more dirty tub!

• **To Banish Ring-Around-the-Tub:** Don't throw out pantyhose that has become unwearable. Instead, use it to get a leg up when it comes to cleaning a ring around the tub. Cut the pantyhose in half and, right after your bath, wad one of the halves into a ball and rub away the ring.

• **To Prevent Rings:** When you take a bath, add two tablespoons of—you guessed it—baking soda to the water, and it should prevent a ring from forming.

• **To Clean Rust Stains:** Combine equal amounts of salt and grapefruit juice. Dip a washcloth in the mixture and have a go at those rust stains.

• **To Get Rid of Chlorinated Water Stains:** Drench paper towels with white vinegar and put them on the water stains. About an hour later, remove the towels, along with the stains.

• **To Fix Discolorations:** Drizzle lemon juice on the discolored spots and leave it there for half an hour. Then, with some baking soda on a wet washcloth, scrub, rinse, dry, and marvel that the spots are gone . . . if they're gone . . . they should be gone . . . we hope they're gone. If they're not, start with a scoop of cream of tartar and add enough hydrogen peroxide to form a paste. Use an old toothbrush to rub the paste into the discolored spots, then let it dry. Once it's dry, rinse it clean.

Folk Belief: Bath Beautification

According to folklore magic, if you bathe in myrtle on April 1, you will

have great beauty and fortune. (Hope this isn't a cruel April Fool's joke.)

SINK

• **To Clean:** All of the (above) bathtub cleaners will also work for the bathroom sink.

DRAINS

• **To Unclog:** A paper clip may be able to fish out some of the hair that is clogging the drain. When you unfold two sides of the clip, you're left with a makeshift hook. Carefully lower it down the drain and try to hook the goop. *Whatever you do, though, don't make matters worse by dropping the clip down the drain!*

In this order, pour 1 cup baking soda, 1 cup salt, and ½ cup vinegar down the drain. Stand back and give the mixture 15 minutes to gurgle its way through the hairy sludge that's down there. Meanwhile, boil 2 quarts water. When the timer goes off, (carefully) pour the just-boiled water down the drain, then let the hot tap water run for 1 minute.

If that doesn't take care of the problem completely, repeat the entire procedure one more time.

• **The Power of Prevention:** There are inexpensive rubber drain covers called "Hair Catchers." They come in two sizes. Before you shop for one, be sure to measure the diameter of the disklike part of your drain that goes up and down to let the water flow or collect.

PLASTIC SHOWER CURTAIN

• **To Prevent Mildew:** Before you hang up a new shower curtain, soak it in salt water, and it should be and stay mildew-free.

• **To Get Rid of Mildew:** If you have a mildewed shower curtain but you're not up to taking it down, sponge it clean with white vinegar.

• **To Wash:** Believe it or not, nowadays most plastic shower curtains can be machine-washed. Be sure to wash your curtain with a couple of bath towels, which will act as buffers against the machine's agitation while scrubbing the curtain clean. Also, add one cup vinegar during the last rinse cycle, and the curtain will come out soft and pliable. Then, you can put the curtain in the dryer *with* the towels, but for only a few minutes, and it will come out wrinkle-free. Don't just stand there reading this, hang it up before it creases!

GLASS SHOWER DOORS

• **To Clean:** After you finish shampooing your hair, pour a little shampoo on a washcloth or sponge and wash the doors. Let the shower spray rinse them. Once you're out of the shower, wipe them dry with your used towel.

For serious grime on the glass doors, apply white vinegar with a damp sponge or washcloth or spritz it on with a spray bottle. Five minutes later, rub a corner of the door with that washcloth as a test patch. If the scum and film come off easily, then continue doing the whole job. If it doesn't get as clean as it should, put baking soda on the washcloth and scour the doors until they're film-free. Then rinse and dry.

SHOWERHEAD

• **Shower Power:** When mineral deposits (hard-water buildup) clog your showerhead and deprive you of a full spray, it's time to do something about it. Pour about a cup of white vinegar in a plastic sandwich bag. Submerge the entire showerhead in the vinegar and, with a thick rubber band or string, secure the bag to the pipe. Let it sit that way overnight, long enough for the vinegar to dissolve the problem. Next morning, debag the showerhead and . . . have a nice spray!

If your showerhead is completely metal and you can detach it from the pipe without doing harm (you'll probably need a wrench to loosen the nut that holds it in place), boil it for about 15 minutes in a mixture of ½ cup vinegar and 1 quart water. Once the head cools off, reattach it.

9

KITCHEN CLEANING

A BASIC CLEANING TOOL

• **Make-It-Yourself Scouring Powder:** Mix 1 cup baking soda and 1 cup borax with ¾ cup salt. Keep a portion of it handy in a large salt shaker, and store the rest in a covered container.

REFRIGERATOR

• **To Deodorize:** Two familiar words . . . baking soda! Keep an open one-pound box on the middle shelf in the back of the refrigerator to absorb odors. It's inexpensive, safe, effective, and, chances are, you already use it. You know, of course, you should replace the box every month or two. Do a good deodorizing deed for your drain by pouring the used soda down the drain while running hot tap water.

Two or three charcoal briquettes will also keep the refrigerator smelling sweet. The economical thing about briquettes is that you can use the same ones over and over. Just heat them in a heavy pot to magically release the absorbed odors, and the briquettes will be like new. Just place them in a dish or open container—a berry lattice-type box—and put them back in the refrigerator.

Several drops of vanilla or lemon extract on cotton balls or in a shot glass in the refrigerator will get rid of bad smells and replace them with a pleasant, clean scent.

When something in the refrigerator spoils and its smell permeates the entire kitchen, crumple brown paper grocery bags and stuff one on each shelf in the fridge. As soon as the bags start smelling bad, replace them. Within a day or two, the paper bags will have absorbed all of the foul odor.

Incidentally, line the vegetable bin with brown paper bags to help keep veggies crisp.

When something smells like a science project gone bad, put fresh coffee grounds in little bowls and place one on each shelf in the fridge. In a couple of days, the odor should be gone and the little bowls removed.

• **To Clean:** Sprinkle baking soda on a damp cloth or sponge. Scrub the fridge surfaces, rinse, and wipe dry.

• **To Shine the Surface:** Dampen a soft cloth with a solution of one part vinegar to five parts water, wash the fridge, rinse and dry, and watch it shine.

STOVE

• **To Clean Oven Spills:** As soon as possible, carefully cover the spill with salt, or wet the spill and cover it with baking soda. When the oven is cool enough to touch, scrape or scour off the spill.

• **To Clean Oven Racks:** Place the oven racks in the bathtub. Fill the tub with very hot water—enough to completely cover the racks. Swish in about ⅓ cup dish detergent and, if the racks have racked up gobs of grease, pour in a cup of white vinegar. (Consider soaking the racks in a heavy-duty plastic bag and save yourself the job of cleaning the bathtub.) After at least an hour of soaking, wipe, rinse, and dry the racks. If some stubborn baked-on grime remains on a rack, carefully scrape it off with a knife.

• **To Clean Burnt-on Food Off a Broiler Pan:** Sprinkle laundry detergent powder on the globs of burnt-on food while the pan is still hot. Then take a water-dampened paper towel and lay it on top of the powdered areas. After about fifteen minutes the food should scrape right off.

• **To Remove Oven-Cleaner Residue:** Okay, so you choose to use a store-bought, air-and-lung-polluting aerosol oven cleaner. Don't you hate the smell and smoke you get when you turn the oven on afterward? To prevent that from happening, in a spray bottle, mix equal parts of white vinegar and water. Spritz the inside of the oven with this vinegar solution, then wipe with a damp cloth or sponge.

• **To Clean Stovetop Spills (see TO CLEAN OVEN SPILLS, above.)**

• **To Clean Gas or Electric Range Surfaces:** Sprinkle baking soda on a damp sponge, scour, rinse, and dry.

• **To Clean Burner Drip Plate and Burner Grate Spills:** In a pot that's *not* aluminum, mix one tablespoon baking soda with one quart water. Boil the stainless steel or enamel burner drip plate for five minutes. When it cools off, wipe it dry. The same remedy applies for cast-iron burner grate spills.

• **Electric-Range Caution:** Do *not* get oven cleaner of any kind, not even baking soda, on the heating elements. Cleanser will cause corrosion, which will result in short-outs.

MICROWAVE

• **To Deodorize:** Lingering food odors will disappear if you combine the juice of a lemon and a cup of water in a microwavable bowl. Place it in the middle of the microwave and heat it to boiling for one minute. Then turn off the oven and let the bowl stay in there for a few minutes more. Now take a whiff, and savor the difference.

• **To Clean:** Do the lemon-and-water number (above), then wipe down the walls with a soap-free sponge or paper towels.

To get those splashes of food cleaned up, sprinkle a little baking soda on a warm, damp cloth, then go at it.

Add one tablespoon baking soda to a cup of warm water and use the mixture to wet a cloth or sponge for a once-a-week microwave wipe-down.

TOASTER

• **To Remove Melted-on Plastic:** Massage petroleum jelly on the plastic splotch. Next, make some toast so that the toaster heats up, then rub off the plastic with a cloth or a paper towel.

Nail-polish remover should remove melted-on plastic from a

toaster. First test an out-of-sight spot to make sure that the polish re-mover won't also remove the toaster's finish.

• **To Clean and Shine:** Gently massage a mixture of equal parts creamy peanut butter and baking soda on the toaster, then wipe it thoroughly with a damp soft cloth.

BLENDER

• **To Clean:** Let the blender container clean itself . . . with a little help from you. After blending a creamy or messy mix, fill one-third with very hot water. Put in a few drops of dish detergent. Before you turn it on, drop in a couple of ice cubes. Don't forget to put the lid on securely. Okay, blend on *high* for a dozen seconds, then rinse re-ally well—unless you want your next *smoothie* to be a *sudsy*.

ELECTRIC CAN OPENER

• **To Keep the Gears Clean:** After using the opener, run a piece of paper towel through the gears to absorb the oil or residue from the just-opened can.

APPLIANCE CHROME

• **To Remove Stains:** Rub the stains with baking soda on a damp cloth.

PORCELAIN SINK

• **To Remove Yellow Stains:** Prepare a paste of three parts cream of tartar to one part hydrogen peroxide, and apply it to the stains. Al-low it to dry, then wipe with a wet cloth or sponge.

STAINLESS-STEEL SINK

• **To Clean:** Baking soda and water! It will clean the sink without scratching it the way an abrasive cleaner would. Be sure to dry the sink to prevent water spots or rust.

• **To Remove Rust and Water Spots:** White vinegar on a damp cloth or sponge will erase the rust and water spots from stainless steel as well as brighten it.

Prepare a paste of three parts cream of tartar to one part hydrogen peroxide, and apply it to the stains. Allow it to dry, then wipe with a wet cloth or sponge.

Rub the surface with rubbing alcohol to remove rust.

Of course, there's always baking soda. Add enough water to a scoop of baking soda to form a thick paste. Put the paste on the stains and leave it for a couple of hours. Then, with a damp cloth, buff the sink, and rinse.

• **To Shine:** Coat the sink with a few drops of baby oil. Wipe it off with paper towels. If it doesn't seem shiny enough, repeat the procedure.

Seltzer or club soda will also help shine up the sink.

• **To Erase Hairline Scratches:** Using very fine steel wool, gently give the entire sink the once-over to obliterate hairline scratches. Then buff with a soft cloth.

FAUCET

• **To Remove Hard-Water Stains:** Wet the blotchy area, sprinkle baking soda on it, put white non-gel toothpaste on an old toothbrush, and brush away the stain.

• **To Remove Hard-Water Buildup** (See SHOWERHEAD at the end of Chapter 8, "Bathroom.")

DRAIN

• **To Degrease and Prevent Clogging:** Pour one cup baking soda and one cup salt down the drain. Follow that with two quarts just-boiled water.

(If it's too late for *preventing* clogs, see DRAINS in Chapter 8, "Bathroom.")

• **To Clean and Freshen:** Pour one cup baking soda and one cup warm vinegar down the drain. Wait ten minutes, then run the hot water for a minute.

DISHWASHER

• **To Clean:** Treat the dishwasher to some Tang. Scatter three to four tablespoons of the orange-drink powder around inside the emptied-out dishwasher and run the wash and rinse cycles. It should get rid of or loosen stains and smell nice, too. Then, when the dishwasher is cool enough to touch, scour off those loosened stains with baking soda.

White vinegar will clean—as well as disinfect—a dishwasher. Pour two to three cups of vinegar in a dishwashable bowl and place it on the lower rack. Run the wash and rinse cycles only. Then open the door and let it air-dry.

GARBAGE DISPOSAL

• **To Deodorize and Sharpen the Blades:** Put peel from a big lemon or two small ones, along with about ten ice cubes (they sharpen the blades), in the garbage disposal compartment. Turn the water on and run the disposal. If you want a shortcut, drop in a teaspoon of lemon juice right after you turn off the disposal.

• **To Prevent Odor:** When you're going to be away from home for a week or more, pour ½ cup baking soda down the disposal—but don't run the water—and come back to an odor-free sink.

• **To Clean:** Every couple of months, take a few minutes to degrease the machine's innards. Simply turn on the hot water in the disposal, then slowly pour in a cup of baking soda. One minute after all the soda is gone, shut the water off.

GARBAGE CAN

• **To Deodorize:** Before you line the can with a plastic bag, sprinkle a light layer of baking soda on the bottom of the can.

CONTAINERS: PLASTIC FOOD HOLDERS, LUNCH BOXES, PITCHERS, ICE CHESTS, ICE BUCKETS, ICE-CUBE TRAYS, THERMOS BOTTLES

• **To Deodorize:** Baking soda should absorb odors from all of the above. There are two ways to use the baking soda. The dry way is to put one or more tablespoons baking soda in the clean-but-smelly container. Close the container and shake it so that the insides are coated. Leave it overnight. Next morning, rinse and let air-dry. The *wet* way (for an I-don't-think-the-smell-will-ever-come-out container) is to fill the container with hot water, equal amounts of baking soda and white vinegar (one or more tablespoons, depending on the size of the container) and a few drops of liquid dish detergent. Cover the container and leave it overnight. In the morning, rinse and air-dry.

Scrunch up newspaper pages and put them in the container, cover it, and leave it overnight. By the following morning, the paper should have absorbed the smell. Wash and dry.

• **To Prevent Plastic-Food-Container Smells:** Line the container with plastic wrap before you put in smelly foods.

• **To Store:** If you're putting away something seasonal, such as an ice chest or picnic containers, scatter a scoop of baking soda in it and it will smell fresh next season when you're ready to use it.

• **To Clean a Thermos Bottle:** Do not soak insulated bottles in water. Instead, mix equal parts cream of tartar and baking soda with enough lemon juice to make a runny paste that will fill one-third of the thermos. Cover, shake, rinse, and dry. To get at a beverage stain on the bottom of the thermos, use a bottle brush or wrap a soft cloth or paper towel around the handle of a wooden spoon, secure it with a rubber band, reach in, and clean.

CUTTING BOARD

• **To Clean and Deodorize:** Sprinkle salt on the cutting board, then rub it with a wedge of lemon or lime.

Of course, baking soda will also clean and remove strong food odors from a cutting board. Scatter baking soda on the board, then spritz it with water. After a few minutes, scrub, rinse, and air-dry—or dry with a clean cloth towel. Clean a rolling pin or wooden bowls the same way.

ROLLING PIN, WOODEN BOWLS
(See CUTTING BOARD above.)

BARBECUE GRILL

• **To Clean** (Same as TO CLEAN OVEN RACKS above.)

Or if this is practical for you, it's worth a try: Place the cooled-off grill on the grass, cooking side down. Leave it overnight, and next morning, see if the *dew* did the job for you. Wipe down the grill with a damp cloth or paper towel. It should be grease-free. Otherwise, use a grill brush *after* you've heated the grill up; the heat will loosen left-over food particles.

COUNTERTOPS

• **To Remove Food Stains:** Make a paste of baking soda and water, cover the stains with it, leave it on for a few minutes, then wipe it off with a damp cloth or sponge.
• **To Remove Purple Ink Stains:** Massage the stain with rubbing alcohol or lemon juice, then wipe with a damp cloth or sponge.
• **Temporary Counter Space:** When your kitchen activity requires more counter space than you have, set up the ironing board. Or you can open a kitchen drawer and put a tray or cutting board or cookie pan on it.

CHINA

• **To Clean Most Stains:** Sprinkle cream of tartar on a damp sponge or cloth and rub the dish clean.

Folk Belief: Break a Wedding Plate

Breaking a plate on one's wedding day is an omen of a future filled with
the best life has to offer a married couple.

• **To Clean Coffee and Tea Stains Off Mugs:** Cream of tartar (above) should work, but if you have a denture-cleaning tablet, you might try filling the mug with warm water and dropping in the tablet. Let it stand overnight and wash it out next morning.

Massage the stained teacup with white non-gel toothpaste, then rinse thoroughly.

• **To Remove a Cigarette Stain:** Drip a couple of drops of water on a scoop of salt, then dip a cork in it. Use the salt-dipped cork to rub away a tobacco stain.

• **To Seal Up a Crack:** Put the cracked dish or cup in a pan with milk and simmer it for about forty to fifty minutes. The protein in the milk should meld the crack together.

POTS AND PANS

• **When Moderately Burned:** Fill the pot with a couple of inches of water and bring it to a boil. Then cover the pot and let it continue boiling for about five minutes. Once it's cool enough to touch, the burn should scour off. If the burns are stubborn, add a few tablespoons baking soda and/or a tablespoon vinegar.

• **To Salvage a Severely Scorched Pan:** Half fill the pan with water and pour in ¼ to ½ cup baking soda, depending on the size of the pan. Let it boil until the burned pieces float on top. Keep a close watch . . . or history will repeat itself.

• **To Salvage a Hopelessly Scorched Pan:** As a last-ditch effort, or as a last effort before you ditch it, fill the pan with mud and leave it for a day. Then use the mud to scour the pan. Hey, you never know.

• **To Clean Aluminum:** Rub a wedge of lemon on the pot and rinse.

• **To Brighten Badly Discolored Aluminum:** Gently boil any of the following: the peel of an apple; slices of grapefruit, lemon, orange, or tomato; or, during rhubarb season, some rhubarb stalks in the pot until the stains vanish. To clean the entire pot, be sure to fill it With as much water as possible.

• **To Clean Copper:** Fill an empty detergent bottle with one part salt and five parts white vinegar and use it on a sponge to clean copper. For stubborn stains, mix equal parts of salt and flour and add enough white vinegar to make a thick paste. With the paste on a sponge or soft cloth, massage the stain, then rinse with hot water.

• **To Remove Tarnish from Copper:** Massage ketchup, Worcestershire sauce, or non-gel toothpaste on copper. If the tarnish doesn't come right off, reapply any of the above and leave it on for half an hour, then wipe off.

• **To Remove Verdigris:** The green patina of copper chloride or copper sulfate that forms on copper can be removed with a paste of lemon juice and baking soda. Apply the paste with a cloth, scour, rinse thoroughly, and buff dry.

• **To Clean Stainless Steel:** Give it the once-over with white vinegar, then sprinkle salt on and massage it with a soft cloth or a paper towel until the dinginess, hairline scratches, and "rainbow" look disappear, leaving behind the shine. Rinse thoroughly and buff dry.

• **To Remove Stains from Nonstick Pans:** Combine two cups water with four tablespoons baking soda in the pan and bring it to a boil. Let it boil for about ten minutes, then wash, rinse, and dry. Before it's used again, reseason the pan by massaging a light layer of vegetable oil on the surface.

• **To Clean Enamel:** If there's food stuck on the bottom of a pot, put in two cups water and a couple of tablespoons baking soda. Then while you do the rest of the dishes, let it boil for about ten minutes. Once it's cool enough to touch, you should be able to scrape off the food, and wash the pot.

• **To Season a New Cast-Iron Pan:** Massage the inside with vegetable or mineral oil and put the pan on the range over a low flame for an hour or in a warm oven (200 degrees) for a couple of hours. As an alternative, you can boil the peel of a couple of potatoes in water in the pan.

The reasoning behind seasoning is to prevent food that's prepared in it from tasting like cast iron. It also helps prevent food from sticking to the pan . . . somewhat.

• **To Clean Burnt Food Off a Cast-Iron Pan:** Fill the pan with water and a little dishwashing detergent, then let it simmer long enough for the globs of food to loosen, then scour them away. Chances are the pan will need to be reseasoned afterward (see TO SEASON A NEW CAST-IRON PAN above).

• **To Remove Rust from a Cast-Iron Pan:** Use steel wool to scour a mixture of sand (available at hardware stores, nurseries, and pet shops) and vegetable oil in your rusty cast-iron pan. Once the rust is gone, wash, then reseason (see TO SEASON A NEW CAST-IRON PAN above).

• **Before Using Clay Cookware for the First Time:** Soak the top and bottom of new clay cookware in water for about one-half hour. Then remove clay dust by scouring with a stiff brush. To prevent food from staining the porous surface and the taste of food from being absorbed, line the cooker with parchment paper.

• **To Remove Stains and Smells from Clay Cookware:** Fill the cooker with water, and, depending on its size, add one to four tablespoons baking soda. Leave it for a few hours, then rinse thoroughly.

• **Clay Cookware No-Nos:** Do not put a hot cooker on a cold counter. Clay cracks.

Do not wash clay cookware in the dishwasher.

Do not scrub clay cookware with steel wool.

COFFEE MAKERS AND TEAKETTLES

• **To Clean Stains on Glass or Stainless-Steel Coffeepots:** Make a paste of three parts baking soda to one part water, and massage the paste into the stains until they're gone. Rinse and dry.

• **To Clean a Glass Coffeepot or Percolator:** Sprinkle salt on a wedge of lemon and massage the pot with it.

Fill the pot with cold water and drop in one denture-cleaning tablet. Let it soak overnight, and rinse in the morning.

• **To Clean a Drip Coffee Maker:** Every few weeks, give the coffee machine a thorough cleaning by pouring equal parts white vinegar and water into the water reservoir and putting it through the brew cycle. Then repeat the brew cycle, but this time use clean water to rinse the machine.

• **To Remove Teakettle Mineral (Lime or Calcium) Deposits:** Fill the kettle with 1 quart water and either ½ cup white vinegar or 2 tablespoons baking soda and 3 tablespoons fresh lemon juice. Boil for about fifteen minutes. When it's cool enough to handle, wash and rinse as usual.

SILVERWARE

(In addition to the following, also check out SILVER in Chapter 1, "General Housekeeping.")

• **The Best Advice:** What are you saving it for? Use it! The more you use "the good stuff," the less it will tarnish and the more beautiful the patina will be.

• **To Prevent Water Spots:** Instead of air-drying, wipe silverware with a lint-free towel.

• **To Prevent Tarnishing or Corroding:** Don't let rubber bands or anything else made of rubber touch silverware or even get close. The sulfur in rubber causes tarnishing and corrosion. Similarly, silverware will tarnish and/or corrode faster when it comes into contact with foods that contain sulfur, like eggs and salad dressing, or mild food acids, such as those found in vinegar, fruit juices, cooked vegetables, salt, and mustard.

• **Washing:** Although silver is dishwasher-proof, Tiffany & Company recommends that silver be washed by hand in hot sudsy water as soon as possible after use, rinsed well in clear hot water, immediately dried thoroughly, and stored absolutely dry. Silverware, especially knives, should never be left to soak in water or air-dry.

• **Dishwasher Warning:** Do not let stainless-steel flatware come in contact with silver in the dishwasher. The electrolytic action that occurs when silver and stainless interact causes pitting on the stainless and leaves black spots on the silver.

• **To Store Silver:** Cleaned and polished silver must be kept dry and away from air. Ideally, you should wrap silverware in specially treated tarnish-proof bags or nontarnishing tissue paper (available at hardware stores). Also available are bags made of "Pacific" cloth, which are very effective in preventing tarnish. Third best are plastic bags. Remember, though, don't secure them with rubber bands.

• **Stainless-Steel Flatware** (See DISHWASHER WARNING above.)

• **To Remove Black Stains from a Stainless-Steel Knife:** Dampen the knife, sprinkle baking soda on the stained areas, then rub it with a cork from a bottle of wine. Rinse and dry. If it has lost its shine, see TO MAKE STAINLESS STEEL SHINE (below).

• **To Remove Rust on a Knife:** Stab an onion with the rusty knife—or any other piece of rusty silverware—and draw the blade in and out a few times. Then leave it in for at least an hour. Wash the knife as usual (throw away the onion).

• **To Make Stainless Steel Shine:** Rub dull flatware with lemon peel.

Spread out the shineless eating utensils in a pan and pour in seltzer or club soda, covering them completely. Leave them until all the fizz is gone. Rinse and dry—marvel at the shine.

GLASSWARE—CRYSTAL

• **To Clean:** Wash with one part white vinegar to three parts water, with or without a little liquid dish detergent. The vinegar cuts grease, eliminates white film on crystal, and leaves glassware sparkling.

Folk Belief: Breaking a Glass Vase

Accidentally breaking a glass or crystal tumbler or vase brings

happiness—seven years of it—and, as a bonus, add to that (in

years), the number of broken pieces. Clearly, it pays to be a klutz.

• **Lint-Free Drying:** Use a linen towel (or one with at least 25 percent linen).

• **To Separate Glasses Stuck Together by Stacking:** Pour cold water in the top glass (contracting it), and submerge the bottom glass in hot water (expanding it).

• **To Pick Up Broken Glass:** Carefully use wet paper towels to collect all the slivers that may have scattered about.

RUBBER GLOVES

• **To Slip On and Off Easily:** Baking soda or talcum powder sprinkled into the gloves will make them glide on—and keep your hands from having that rubber-glove smell. Go easy on the sprinkling, though. A little goes a long way.

• **When Gloves Get Wet on the Inside:** If they're wet inside because they've sprung holes, there's not much you can do. If they're wet because water seeped in through the cuff, try this: Right before you take them off, thoroughly dry the outside. Then, pull them off by the cuff so that you can turn them inside out. Be sure that each finger is completely inside out. Let them air-dry. Then you're ready to turn them back and wear them—after sprinkling in a little powder.

STEEL WOOL

• **To Prevent Rusting:** Right after you finish using a steel-wool pad, put it in a plastic bag and store it in the freezer until you need to use it again. It may be cold, but it won't be rusty. Warm water thaws the pad in seconds.

• **A Clever Steel-Wool Holder:** Protect your fingers when using steel wool by cupping and holding the pad with the skin of a scooped-out half of an orange or lemon.

SPONGES

• **To Deodorize:** A sponge will absorb and hold on to food odors. In a bowl, dissolve three tablespoons salt in two cups hot water. Submerge the sponge and keep it in place by putting a glass on top of it. Leave it overnight and rinse it odor-free in the morning.

• **To Refresh and Disinfect:** Drench a stinky sponge with lemon juice, then rinse it out thoroughly.

BABY HIGH CHAIR

• **To Clean:** After every meal, wash down the serving tray—and whatever other surface was splattered—with baking soda on a damp cloth or sponge. The rest of the high chair should get the once-over with a solution of two tablespoons baking soda in one pint water.

MOVING LARGE KITCHEN APPLIANCES

• **To Clean Behind or Under:** Move something big and heavy—like a refrigerator or dishwasher—by smearing butter or any other shortening on the floor right in front of the appliance. That should make it easier for you to slide it out—with someone helping, of course.

JARS

• **To Remove Labels:** Massage mayonnaise into the label, then let the jar soak in hot water. Within minutes you should be able to peel off the label.

Dip a cotton swab in nail-polish remover and rub it over the label. Keep dipping and rubbing until the label is off.

• **To Remove Price Tag or Label Glue:** Work peanut butter into the sticky spot until all the glue is off.

CONTACT PAPER

• **To Make It Easy to Work With:** Put contact paper in the freezer for at least an hour before using it. Then line shelves or drawers with it to your heart's content.

• **To Remove:** Run a warm iron over the shelf paper, and it should peel off without a problem.

10

KITCHEN STUFF

ALUMINUM FOIL

• **What Not to Wrap:** Foods containing natural acids—tomatoes, onions, lemons—should not be wrapped in foil. A chemical reaction caused by the combination of acid and foil can affect the taste of the food. Use plastic wrap instead.

Salty foods can cause foil to rust.

BAKING

• **Oven Setting:** Preheat the oven for about ten minutes at the degrees called for in the recipe, so that by the time you start baking, the oven will be evenly heated at the required setting.

BOTTLES

• **To Empty Quickly:** When you're washing a lot of bottles and want to get it over with, you can speed up the slowest part—waiting for the water to empty out of each bottle—by turning the bottles upside down and giving them each a few shakes in a circular motion. You'll be creating a whirlpool effect, with the air rushing in and the water flowing out.

CANDLES

• **To Position Properly:** Always keep candles in draft-free places. Drafts from an open window or door, air conditioner, or fans will cause candles to drip (yes, even the costly dripless variety) and burn twice or three times as fast as they should.

COUPONS

• **Don't Leave Home Without 'Em:** To make sure you remember to take those money-saving coupons with you, write your grocery shopping list on the back of an envelope in which you place all the coupons you need for that list.

CREATIVE CANDLESTICKS

Carve out openings in apples, little pumpkins, oranges, grapefruits, mini-watermelons, or whatever other edible is appropriate for the meal, and insert your candles. Use several as a unique centerpiece, or put one at each place setting.

DOUBLE BOILER

• **To Prevent Burnouts:** Put a few marbles into the water in the bottom of a double boiler. If the water level should get alarmingly low, the marbles will make enough noise to bring your attention to it.

Folk Belief: Green Candle Dividends

Burn a green candle and don't be surprised if you get money

from an unexpected source. And if that's not enough luck, your

plants will benefit, too, by growing better.

FREEZER

• **For Efficient Freezing:** Since foods keep the cold in a freezer better than air does, it's best and most economical to keep the freezer as full as possible. Fill in the empty spaces with plastic bottles of water, or make extra and unusual ice cubes (see ICE CUBES in Chapter 11, "Food.")

When you're putting a warm item in the freezer, try not to put it near an already-frozen food that you wouldn't want to absorb the heat. Instead, place it near the ice cubes.

Do not wrap food that you want to freeze in already-used aluminum foil. The previous crinkling of the foil may have created little holes that will let air in and increase the chance of freezer burn or spoilage.

• **To Freeze in Plastic Bags** (See AIR-FREE under PLASTIC BAGS below.)

• **Date and Label:** You think you'll remember what and when you put things in the freezer. Well, maybe you will, but date and label everything anyway.

• **Defrosting Assistance:** Use a baster that's filled with hot water to help melt frozen-solid food items.

• **Defrosting Made Easier:** When you defrost the freezer, wipe it dry, then spray it with nonstick vegetable spray. It should make the next defrosting somewhat easier.

• **To Deodorize:** When the freezer has an unpleasant food smell, put half a cup of fresh-ground coffee on a dish and place the dish in the freezer. Give it a couple of days for the coffee to completely absorb the odors.

JARS

• **To Get a Tightened Lid Off:** Get a grip with rubber—either wear rubber gloves or put a thick rubber band around the rim of the lid—and twist.

Turn the jar upside down and hold it under hot tap water for a minute. When you turn the jar right side up, you should be able to twist open the lid.

KNIVES

• **To Sharpen:** Until you get a *real* sharpener, try rubbing the blade on the bottom of a terra-cotta flowerpot.

LUNCH BOX

• **To Keep Cool:** Take a frozen box or can of fruit juice in your lunch box, and it will keep the sandwich and fruit cool until you're ready to eat. By then, the juice will have thawed and you'll be able to enjoy the drink with lunch.

MICROWAVE

• **Plastic Wrap:** Use only plastic wrap that's labeled "microwavable."
• **For Safety's Sake:** When you take a plastic-wrapped dish out of the microwave, start removing the plastic wrap by folding back the side that's farthest away from you. By so doing, you will be out of the line-of-fire from the first burst of scalding-hot steam that puffs out.
• **To Test for Microwavability:** Place the test container in the microwave alongside a cup that's half filled with water. Zap it on *high* for one minute. If the container in question is cool, then it's *cool* to use it in the microwave; if it's warm, you can use it to reheat . . . cautiously; if it's hot, *don't!* It's *not* to be used in the microwave.

NONSTICK SPRAY

• **Make Your Own:** In a pump bottle, combine equal parts of vegetable oil and liquid lecithin (available at health-food stores).

ODORS

• **To Keep It Local:** Place a pail of cold water at the kitchen door to keep unpleasant cooking odors from wafting into other rooms.
    (See TO DEODORIZE in FREEZER above.)
    (See REFRIGERATOR in Chapter 9, "Kitchen Cleaning.")

PICNICS

• **Seasoning Holders:** Fill paper straws with salt, pepper, oregano, garlic powder, or any other seasoning you desire. Since most funnels aren't small enough to fit in a straw, just stick the straw into the jar of seasoning and it will fill itself. Twist the ends closed, or bend the ends down and secure them with rubber bands, and you have portable, disposable shakers.

• **Pest-Proof Beverages:** To keep insects from taking the plunge into your drink, sculpt a piece of aluminum foil across the top of your glass or cup and hold it in place with a rubber band. Then stick a straw through the foil.

PLASTIC BAGS

• **Air-Free:** When freezing food in a plastic bag, you want as little air as possible in the bag. To reduce the amount of air, use a Ziploc bag. Insert a straw in the bag, then zip it closed as far it will go. Using the straw, suck out the air from the bag, then, in one fell swoop, remove the straw and zip the bag closed.

• **Filling the Bag:** The easy way to fill a supermarket's plastic produce bag with a bulky vegetable (like broccoli) is to put your hand in the bag, grab hold of the veggie with that bagged hand, and with your other hand pull the bag over the vegetable. If the bag has printing on it, be sure to turn it inside out first, because the printing may contain lead, and you don't want that touching anything you're going to eat.

PLASTIC CONTAINERS

• **To Prevent Stains:** Before you pour leftover tomato sauce—or anything else that may be hard to wash out—into a plastic container, spray the container with nonstick vegetable spray.

RECIPES

• **A Neat Idea:** Use a photo album as a recipe book. Each time you cut a recipe out of a newspaper or magazine, place it in one of the album's plastic sleeves. That sleeve will shield it from drips and spatters when you use the recipe.

• **Cookbook Protection:** Instead of messing up the cookbook page you're working from, put the book in a clear plastic bag or wrap plastic wrap around it.

• **Be Prepared to Tape:** If you have a VCR and know how to operate it, always have a tape ready in the machine. That way, you'll get recipes you want without having to send a SASE (self-addressed stamped envelope) or a check for a transcript. Right then and there, you'll have the recipe, with the live demonstration.

REFRIGERATOR

• **Cost Considerations:** According to Con Edison in New York City, a twenty-year-old, fourteen-cubic-foot, frost-free refrigerator costs about $26 a month to run. A new, energy-efficient model costs about $9.25 monthly. Lesson? It may pay to invest in a new fridge.

• **To Save on Electricity:** Don't dawdle in front of the refrigerator's open door. Know what you want, open the door, get it, and get out. When you want to put away groceries, gather them together before you open the door.

• **To Store Food:** Make sure that all foods are covered. That way, the food won't dry out or take on a refrigerator smell, and the refrigerator won't have to use up extra energy to keep up with the extra moisture emitted by uncovered food.

• **The Br-r-r-r Spot:** If you want to keep something *really* cold— or if you want a hot dish to cool down quickly—put it in the refrigerator's coldest spot, the back of the top shelf.

• **Ideal Conditions:** For a refrigerator to perform most efficiently, air should be able to circulate around each container on the shelves. In other words, don't overload.

• **Leftovers:** Consider putting leftovers in glass jars so you can be reminded of their existence. It's also a good idea, though not always practical, to keep leftovers in one designated section of the fridge so you don't forget about them.

SCALE

• **To Test for Accuracy:** Put nine pennies on your kitchen scale If they weigh one ounce, the scale is accurate.

SHOPPING

• **The Order of Things:** Arrange your shopping list so that the last items you put in the cart are the ones that need to be refrigerated—meat, fish, poultry, dairy products, ice cream and frozen foods. You may want to ask that they be bagged together. Be sure to refrigerate them the second you get home.

STRAINER

• **To Strain Liquid:** If you don't have a *fine* strainer, create one by lining a colander with a few layers of dampened cheesecloth or a piece of nylon from an unusable, clean pair of pantyhose. What? You don't have a colander? Punch holes in an aluminum pie plate. If you don't have a pie plate, we hope you have a *fine* strainer.

TABLE SETTING

• **Quick Reminder of the Basics:** Forks are on the left; knives—cutting side toward the plate—and spoons are on the right. The pieces of silverware (maximum: three on each side of the plate) should be placed in order of use, starting from the outside. For instance, on the left: the fork for the appetizer, the fork for the salad, and next to the plate, the fork for the entrée; on the right: the soup-spoon, the teaspoon and the knife. The goblet or water glass should be on the right of the plate, at the tip of the knife.

Folk Belief: Dropped Silverware

You may already know that if you drop silverware you can

expect company. But do you know who? If you drop a knife, it will be

a man; a fork, a woman; and a spoon, a baby.

11

FOOD

ANCHOVIES

• **To Reduce Saltiness:** Soak them in cold water for about fifteen minutes. Strain out the water and pat dry with a paper towel. If they're still too salty, soak them again. If they're *still* too salty, you probably don't like anchovies. Find something else to eat!

APPLES

• **To Keep Cut Apples from Turning Brown:** Spritz the cut apples with the juice of an orange, grapefruit, or lemon. Or mix ¼ teaspoon salt in 1 pint water and dunk the cut pieces of apple in it.
• **To Store:** Apples stay longest in a cool, dark place, like the refrigerator fruit bin. Since it seems to be true about one bad apple spoil-

Folk Belief: Baked Apple Goodness

If an apple bursts while it's baking in the oven, the cook

can expect good news soon.

ing the rest, it's best—though not too practical—to place apples in the fruit bin so that they don't touch each other.

• **For a Better-Looking Baked Apple:** Before you bake, remove ½ inch of peel around the apple, letting its midriff show through. That horizontal opening will allow steam to escape and prevent the rest of the peel from splitting.

ASPARAGUS

• **Its Staying Power:** Asparagus will keep for about three days. It's best, however, to eat it the day you get it. Wash it right before you prepare it, however, not the minute you get home.

• **To Store:** Stand spears in about an inch of cold water and cover with a plastic bag.

• **To Revive Limp Spears:** Cut a quarter inch off the ends, stand the spears in a couple of inches of ice water, cover with a plastic bag, and refrigerate for about two hours.

• **To Remove the Woody Portion:** Hold the spear with both hands as though you were going to snap it in half. And do just that, snap it—but not in half. Snap it closer to the end, at the point where it breaks off naturally. The spear will let you know the part that's too tough to be eaten.

• **To Open Canned Asparagus:** If you open the *top* of an asparagus can and spill out the spears tips first, you're likely to damage them. Open the *bottom* of the can, and the tips will glide out last in top-tip shape.

AVOCADOES

• **To Speed Up the Ripening Process:** Place the avocado in a brown paper bag with a tomato or a banana peel. Close the bag and store it in a warmish place, but keep checking the avocado's firmness so you don't allow it to get overripe.

• **To Keep Cut Avocado from Browning:** Exposure to oxygen causes the meat to turn brown. Leave the pit in place, brush on lemon juice, then lock out air by covering the cut half with plastic wrap and refrigerate. The same goes for guacamole.

BACON

• **To Separate Slices:** Right before you use the bacon, put it in the microwave and zap it on *high* for about thirty seconds. For those of you without a microwave, when you bring home the bacon, roll the entire package lengthwise, secure it with rubber bands, and refrigerate it. When you're ready to use it, the bacon slices will peel apart easily.

• **To Minimize Shrinkage:** Don't preheat the skillet. Just put the bacon in and cook it over a medium flame.

• **To Prevent Curling:** Before frying, rinse the slices in cold water.

• **To Prevent Splattering:** Toss a few celery leaves in with the bacon to put an end to grease spurting. Or, while frying, continually remove the liquid grease with a meat baster. That will lessen the splattering and make the bacon crisper.

• **Shelf Life:** Once you open a package of sliced bacon, it should last up to a week in the fridge.

BAGELS

• **To Freeze Bagels:** Slice them in half before you put them in the deep freeze. You'll be glad you did, especially when you want them to defrost quickly, or when you want to toast them frozen.

BANANAS

• **To Speed the Ripening Process:** Poke some air holes in a brown paper bag, then put the unpeeled, unripe bananas in, along with a ripe apple. Check daily that you're not allowing them to become overripe.

• **To Prevent Peeled Bananas from Browning:** Brush the bananas with orange or lemon juice.

• **To Store:** Put unpeeled ripe bananas in a sealed jar or a plastic bag (with as little air as possible), and refrigerate. The peel will turn brown, but the meat of the banana will be fine.

• **For a Frozen Snack:** Wrap a peeled, ripe banana in aluminum foil and freeze it. When you feel like having a low-calorie, dairy-free

Folk Belief: Lucky Bananas

Before you eat the next banana, make a wish. Then cut a coin-sized slice

from the end of the banana that was attached to the stalk. If you can find

the shape of a Y in the slice of banana, your wish will come true.

treat, take off the foil and eat the banana as you would a Popsicle. If you have a heavy-duty blender or juicer, toss frozen banana pieces in and whip up a delicious banana custard.

BEANS

• **To Cook Dried Beans:** Add salt *after* you've finished cooking the beans. Cooking time will be reduced—and so will the amount of salt used for seasoning.

• **To Reduce the Gaseous Effect of Cooked Beans:** Soak beans in water overnight with a teaspoon of fennel seeds tied up in a piece of cheesecloth. In the morning, remove the fennel seeds and use fresh water to cook the beans. While the beans are cooking, throw in a few pieces of potatoes. When the beans are ready, take out the potato, and enjoy.

Another degasser is to let the beans simmer for about twenty minutes, *carefully* pour out the water, and replace it with the same amount of fresh boiling water.

• **To Prevent Boiling Over:** Add a tablespoon of vegetable oil to the cooking water. We just discovered an inexpensive Boil-Over Preventer at a houseware store. It's a glass disk that sits on the bottom of the pot and reduces the amount of water that boils over. It's worth a buy—and a try.

• **To Store Insect-Free:** A dried hot pepper in the bean container will repel weevils and other insects.

BREAD AND OTHER
BREADBASKET FILLERS

• **To Cut Fresh Bread:** A warmed-up knife, inserted in a glass of just-boiled water, will cut fresh bread more efficiently.

• **To Store:** Wrap bread, pita, English muffins, rolls, bagels, crackers, or breadsticks in plastic bags that are as airtight as possible. The refrigerator will dry out these bread items, so it's better to leave them at room temperature or to freeze them.

• **To Freshen Stale Bread:** Wrap the loaf in aluminum foil with as little air as possible, then let it bake in a 250-degree oven for about ten minutes.

• **To Rebake Stale Rolls or Muffins:** Wet a small brown paper bag and put the stale rolls in it. Put the bag in a 300-degree oven. In only a few minutes, when the bag is dry, the rolls will taste freshly baked.

Spritz rolls or muffins with water, wrap loosely in aluminum foil, and put them in an oven at 350-degrees for ten to fifteen minutes. You'll be surprised at how just-baked they will taste. If you're warming a croissant-type crusty roll, put it in the oven uncovered.

• **For a Shiny Surface on Baked Bread:** Brush the top with white vinegar about five minutes before it has finished baking.

• **For Higher, Lighter Whole-Wheat Bread:** Add one table-spoon lemon juice while mixing the dough, and the bread will rise higher and be lighter. And, no, you won't taste the lemon.

• **To Serve Bread:** Line the breadbasket with aluminum foil and cover the foil with a napkin. That way, warm bread and rolls will stay warm longer.

BREAD CRUMBS

• **To Prepare Your Own:** Lightly toast bread, tear it in pieces, and put it in the blender or processor. You can also season it with crushed dried herbs and powdered spices to taste.

• **Bread-Crumb Substitutes:** Use ¾ cup cracker crumbs for every cup of bread crumbs called for in a recipe.

Folk Belief: Bread Breaking and Baking

To break bread together is to share friendship. Bread, regarded as a holy

substance, is to be respected and must not be jabbed with a fork

or knife while it's being baked.

Try whole-grain flaked cereals, like bran, in place of bread crumbs for stuffing, as a casserole topping, or as a filler for meatloaf and veggie burgers.

BUTTER

• **To Prevent Burning:** One minute it's fine, half a minute later it's burnt and black. Next time, when sautéing in butter, add a little olive oil. The combination will keep the butter from burning.

BUTTERMILK

• **Substitute in Baking:** When the recipe calls for buttermilk, you can substitute the same quantity of plain yogurt.

Another buttermilk substitute is one tablespoon lemon juice or one tablespoon white vinegar mixed into one cup milk. Let it stand for ten minutes, then use.

CABBAGE

• **To Wash Away Insects:** Fill a basin with cold water, add a couple of tablespoons white vinegar, and soak the cabbage in it. This should wash out any small insects that may be hiding between the leaves.

Folk Belief: Cabbage Before Bed

Pliny, the Roman scholar and naturalist, advised eating cabbage

before going to sleep to prevent nightmares.

- **To Reduce the Smell of Cooking:** As soon as you start cooking cabbage, drop a walnut—shell and all—into the pot.
  Add ½ lemon to the water when boiling.
  Add a pinch of baking soda or a stalk of celery.
  Place a heel of bread on top of the cabbage while it's cooking.
- **To Pull Off the Leaves Easily:** Put the head of cabbage in the freezer until it's completely frozen. Then let it thaw out. The leaves will soften and be easy to pull apart.

CAKE

- **To Prevent a Cake from Sticking:** Before placing a cake on a cake plate, sprinkle the plate with powdered sugar.
- **A Fat Substitute:** That's right . . . a substitute for fat when baking some—though not all—cakes. The secret ingredient is applesauce as an even-quantity substitute for oil, butter, or margarine. This applesauce substitute seems to work best in recipes that include wet ingredients such as fruit or milk. Considering the fat grams and calories you can save, it's worth experimenting with, especially if you're a health-conscious eater.
- **To Cut a Frosted Cake:** Wet the knife with hot water and you'll slice the cake more easily and neatly.
- **To Cut Cheesecake:** Use a piece of unflavored dental floss that's a little longer than the diameter of the cake. With an end in each hand, hold the floss taut and cut the cake in half, sliding the floss out

from the bottom. Then, after separating the two halves, use the same method to cut a slice at a time.

• **To Decorate an Unfrosted Cake:** After the cake has cooled, place a round paper doily on top of the cake, and sprinkle confectioner's sugar on it—enough to fill in all the openings in the doily's pattern. Then carefully lift the doily off the cake, and you're left with an elegant cake that looks as if it's from the Victorian era. If you're creative, you can cut patterns from a sheet of paper and make your own doily.

• **To Test a Cake:** When a toothpick isn't long enough to test the doneness of a cake, a stick of uncooked spaghetti will do the same job.

• **To Evenly Distribute Fruits and Nuts:** Put raisins and other dried fruit pieces and/or nuts in a plastic bag, add a little flour, and shake so that they get flour-coated. Then when you add them to your cake batter, they won't all settle on the bottom.

• **The Easy Way to Mix Dry Ingredients:** When baking a cake, put all the dry ingredients in a plastic or paper bag and shake.

• **Nonstick Substitute:** After greasing a pan, instead of sprinkling it with flour, use wheat germ. It will prevent the cake from sticking and is a lot healthier than flour

CANDY

• **When to Make Candy:** Since sugar blots up humidity, candy made on rainy or damp days will not set properly. Choose dry days to play Fanny Farmer.

• **To Prevent Candy-Making Boilover:** Butter an inch around the inside of the top of the pot when boiling candy.

CAULIFLOWER

• **To Wash Away Insects:** Float out little bugs by soaking the head of cauliflower in ice water with the florets facing down.

• **To Keep Its Color While Cooking:** Cook the cauliflower with the florets facedown, and add a teaspoon of white vinegar or a little milk to the water.

CELERY

• **To Remove Strings:** Simply peel stalks with a potato peeler and there will be no strings attached.

• **To Store:** Put the stalks in a paper bag and don't remove the leaves until you're ready to use them.

• **To Recrisp Rubbery Celery:** Put the stalks in a bowl or pickle dish with ice water and raw potato slices. After about an hour, the celery should be revived.

CHAMPAGNE

• **How Much and What It's Called:** According to the prestigious Champagne Wines Information Bureau, for a champagne apéritif at cocktail hour, allow one bottle for every three or four guests. When serving at a meal, count on one bottle for every two or three people. And for the traditional champagne toast to the bride, stretch one bottle to serve six to ten people.

The following may help you place your order.

Split	½ pint
Half	1 pint
Bottle	1 quart
Magnum	2 quarts
Jeroboam	4 quarts
Rehoboam	6 quarts
Methuselah	8 quarts
Salmanazar	12 quarts
Balthazar	16 quarts
Nebuchadnezzar	20 quarts

• **How to Open:** No one knows better than the Champagne Wines Information Bureau. Here's what they advise: Slant the bottle at a 45-degree angle away from guests. With a thumb on the cork, untwist and loosen the wire muzzle. Grasp the cork firmly, twist the bottle slowly, and let the pressure help push out the cork. Allow a light and merry pop.

Folk Belief: Bottle's Last Drop

If a single person drinks the last drop in a bottle, it means

wedding bells within the year; if the last-drop drinker

is married, a child will be on the way.

In case you didn't already know, the pressure in a bottle of champagne is equivalent to that of a tire of a London double-decker bus—about ninety pounds per square inch.

• **Seasonal Panache:** For that special winter evening, chill the champagne in an ice bucket filled with snow.

• **To Prepare for Serving:** Refrigerate champagne for only about two to three hours before serving. Longer than that, and you risk weakening the taste and bouquet.

• **How to Prevent Bubbling Over as You Pour:** First time around, fill each glass about one-third of the way, then go back and double the amount. That way you allow the fizzing to go down, and you end up with a glass that is appropriately two-thirds full.

CHEESE

• **To Store Cottage or Ricotta Cheese:** Once the containers have been opened, keep them upside down in the refrigerator. They will stay fresher longer that way. We don't know why, but it works.

Transfer the cheese to a small glass jar with a screw-on lid and refrigerate.

• **To Prevent Mold on Hard Cheese:** Wrap the piece of cheese in a cloth that's been dampened with apple cider vinegar, then seal it in a plastic bag. The acid in the vinegar will ward off mold.

• **To Bring Out the Flavor:** Zap hard cheese in a microwave for about fifteen seconds on a medium setting. You'll taste the difference.

Folk Belief: Poultry Wish

Let a wishbone dry for a day or two until it's brittle. You take one

end and have someone else take the other end. Each makes a wish

and pulls the bone apart. The person who gets the longer piece

will have his wish granted.

CHICKEN

• **For Extra Crispy:** By adding one rounded tablespoon cornstarch for each cup of flour, your fried chicken will be the crispiest ever.

CHOCOLATE

• **Baking Substitute:** When a recipe calls for squares of unsweetened chocolate and you're out of them, you can substitute three tablespoons cocoa and one tablespoon shortening for each square.

Folk Belief: Chocolate Dreams

It is said that if you eat chocolate right before you go to sleep, you will

have wonderful, romantic dreams. That's reason enough to eat the chocolate

left on the pillow in a hotel room.

CINNAMON

• **Give Your Home a Pleasant Scent:** Everyone loves the comforting, nostalgic smell of cinnamon. Real-estate agents advise clients to have the aroma of cinnamon in the air when showing their homes—they sell faster that way.

Of course, you can do this without selling your home: Stir two teaspoons ground cinnamon or a few cinnamon sticks into a saucepan with two cups water, and let it simmer on a low flame. The lovely scent will waft its way through many rooms.

COCONUT

• **To Open a Coconut:** There are three eyes—small black spots—on the coconut. With a large nail and a hammer, pierce the eyes and pour out the milk. Then put the coconut in a 375-degree oven for half an hour. As soon as it cools, it may crack by itself. If not, gently tap on it with the hammer.

COFFEE

• **To Store:** If you use ground coffee or coffee beans only occasionally, keep them in the freezer so that they keep their strong flavor.

Folk Belief: Bubbles in Your Coffee

Legend has it that money will come to you if there are bubbles in your first cup of coffee of the day. If the bubbles are on the side of the cup from which you drink, the money will come soon; if the bubbles are on the far side, it will be a while before you can quit your day job.

• **Coffee Filter Substitute:** A substantial paper napkin or two paper towels should fill in for a filter. It's worth a try if you really need that cup of coffee.

• **Recycle Leftover Coffee:** Fill an ice-cube tray with leftover coffee and freeze it. You'll probably think of many ways to use the coffee cubes. We'll start you off with a couple: Cool piping-hot coffee with a couple of cubes. Make iced coffee faster and stronger with these cubes. Okay, now you're on your own.

COOKIES

• **For Nonstick Plopping:** Dip the spoon in milk before scooping up cookie dough with it. The milk should enable the dough to plop from the spoon to the cookie sheet without sticking. If you use your hands to shape the cookies, keep wetting them with cold water for a smoother release.

• **No More Cookie-Sheet Cleanup:** Instead of greasing a cookie sheet, line it with baking parchment paper. It's wonderful stuff. The cookies bake more evenly and you don't have to clean the cookie sheet.

• **To Cut Bar Cookies:** Use a pizza cutter for neat, smooth squares.

• **To Keep Cookies from Drying Out:** Put a piece of apple in the cookie jar to keep cookies moist.

• **To Keep Cookies Soft:** Keep a slice of bread in the cookie jar.

• **To Keep Cookies Crisp:** Scrunch up a sheet of tissue paper and put it on the bottom of the cookie jar, then put the cookies on top of the tissue. Always put the lid back on.

CORN

• **To Select an Ear:** Look for corn with husks. They will have the most flavor. Check for freshness by looking at the bottom of the ear. If it's brown or dry, or if the leaves at the top are shriveled, the corn is probably old. (To tell when an ear of corn is ripe, see CORN in Chapter 14, "Gardening.")

• **To Remove Corn Silk:** With a damp paper towel, wipe off the silken threads in a downward motion.

• **To Remove Kernels from the Cob:** Use a (clean) shoehorn as you would a knife to scrape the kernels off the corn. Isn't that a great idea? A shoehorn!

CORNSTARCH

• **Substitute:** When a recipe calls for cornstarch and you don't have any, use twice the called-for quantity of flour in its place.

CUCUMBER

• **To Store:** Keep cukes in the warmest place in the fridge—the vegetable bin on the bottom shelf. When they get too cold, they get mushy.

DRIED FRUIT

• **Nonstick Cutting:** Cutting dried fruit with a wet knife will prevent the pieces from sticking.
   Spray a pair of kitchen scissors with a nonstick vegetable spray before cutting.
• **To Distribute Evenly in Cake.** (See CAKE above.)

EGGS

• **To Store:** The second you walk in the door from the supermarket, refrigerate the eggs. Every hour that they're at room temperature is said to be equivalent to a week in the fridge.
• **To Keep Fresh Longer:** Don't wash them before putting them in the refrigerator. And don't put them in the door of the fridge (even though most models have egg receptacles in the door). They should be kept in the egg carton they came in to prevent moisture from escaping. Oh, and one more thing: line the eggs up pointed side down.
• **To Test Freshness:** Put a raw egg in a pot of water. A fresh egg will sink and lie on its side; an egg that tilts is at least three or four days old; if it stands on its pointy end, we're talking ten days to two weeks old; if an egg floats, it's rotten.

Folk Belief: Standing Eggs

During the spring equinox on or about March 21, the sun shines

directly on the equator, and the length of the day is the same as the length

of the night all over the world.

The ancient Chinese created a ritual of standing eggs upright at the spring

equinox for good luck. On that one day a year for about a fifteen-minute

period, eggs, the Chinese symbol of fertility, can stand on end.

• **To Separate the White from the Yolk:** Place a small funnel in a glass, then crack the egg over the funnel. While the yolk will stay in the top part of the funnel, the white part will glide into the glass.

• **Raw or Hard-Boiled, a Test:** Spin the egg. A hard-boiled egg will spin; a raw one will just wobble around.

• **To Prevent Cracking While Boiling:** Before putting the egg in the water, carefully puncture the pointed end with a pin.

Add a teaspoon of white vinegar to the water.

• **To Peel a Hard-Boiled Egg:** Peeling is easiest when the egg is still hot. To start, crack it on the rounded end where there's an air bubble. If the shell doesn't come right off, peel the egg under cold running water.

• **Substitutes:** If a recipe calls for an egg and you are cholesterol-conscious, use the cholesterol-free whites of two eggs in place of one whole egg. (The leftover yolk makes a super face mask.)

• **To Keep Yolks:** Combine yolks with cold water in a covered container and refrigerate. They'll stay fresh that way for days.

• **Egg Substitute:** When a recipe calls for several eggs and you're short one, use a teaspoon of cornstarch in its place. Or, when baking

Folk Belief: Egg Visitors

If an egg cracks while it's being boiled, it is believed that

unexpected visitors will be arriving soon.

a cake, use one teaspoon white vinegar and one teaspoon baking soda mixed together.

FAT

• **Deep-Fat Frying:** Before heating the fat, add one tablespoon white vinegar to minimize the amount of fat absorbed by the frying food. The food will also taste less greasy.

FISH

• **To Determine Cooking Time:** Lay down the whole fish, fish steak, or fillet, and, with a ruler, measure its thickness at the thickest part. Figure ten minutes cooking time for each inch of thickness.

• **To Thaw:** Put frozen fish in milk. The milk will remove the freezer taste and allow it to cook up as though it were fresh.

• **To Enhance the Taste:** Put about two tablespoons white vinegar in a bowl with water and soak the fish in it for about fifteen minutes before cooking. This process will make it seem fresher, less fishy, and tastier, too.

• **To Prevent Frying-Fish Smell:** Put a teaspoon of peanut butter in the pan while frying fish, and guests won't guess what you're preparing. The peanut butter will also add a touch more taste.

Place a small bowl of white vinegar or fresh coffee grounds next to the stove to help absorb the cooking odors.

• **To Deodorize the Pan:** After cooking fish, wash the pan with white vinegar to get rid of the fishy smell.

• **To Remove the Fishy-Oil Taste of Canned Fish:** Drizzle a little white vinegar in an opened can of tuna or sardines, and after a few minutes, spill it out, along with all that fishy-oil taste.

FLOUR

• **To Store for Handy Retrieval:** Fill a big salt shaker with flour and keep it in the freezer. It will save you the trouble of dealing with the unwieldy sack of flour each time you want to dust a work surface or coat chicken with it.

If you keep flour in a canister, toss a never-used powder puff in, too. What easier way to dust a rolling pin, pan, or whatever needs a light coat of flour?

• **To Store:** The ideal place to store flour is in the freezer, where it stays fresh and bug-free.

• **Flour Substitute for Flour:** As a substitute for 1 cup all-purpose flour, you can use 1 cup and 2 tablespoons cake flour. As a substitute for 1 cup cake flour, use 1 cup minus 2 tablespoons all-purpose flour. As a substitute for 1 cup self-rising flour, combine 1½ teaspoons baking powder with ½ teaspoon salt, and fill up the rest of the (level) cup with all-purpose flour.

FRUIT
(See TO REMOVE PESTICIDES below under VEGETABLES.)

GARLIC

• **To Peel:** Put a clove on its side on a counter or cutting board. Put the flat side of a wide knife's blade on top of the clove. Make a fist, then WHAM! Pound down on the knife that's on the clove. A gentler method is to press down with the heel of your hand. In both cases, the peel should come right off. Incidentally, if you use a garlic press, the garlic will be squeezed through its skin, so there's no need to peel it.

Folk Belief: Good Luck Garlic

Known for keeping vampires away, a bunch of garlic bulbs on

or hanging over your living-room mantel is also believed to bring lots of

good luck. (Be sure to replace the garlic every month.)

• **A Garlic Spread:** It's easy to roast garlic, and once you do, there are dozens of uses for it, each one delicious. Start with a bulb of garlic and slough off the outer layers of skin. Then pull apart all the cloves and put them on a square piece of aluminum foil that's big enough to loosely enclose the cloves. Take one teaspoon olive oil and drip a drop or two on each clove. Bring the corners of the foil to the center, loosely wrapping the cloves, then pinch closed every opening of the foil. Bake at 400 degrees for about thirty minutes, until the cloves are soft. To test, puncture a clove with the tip of a knife.

Use it as you would butter on baked or mashed potatoes, or spread it on Italian bread. Better yet, make it, taste it, and be inspired to come up with your own ways to enhance a meal.

Roasted cloves can be refrigerated in an airtight container for a week or more.

• **In the Microwave:** Garlic loses some of its potency when cooked in a microwave. You might want to consider increasing the amount of garlic in a microwave-prepared dish.

• **To Smell Kissing Sweet:** If, while you're cooking, you sample a garlicky treat, drink a little lemon juice mixed with some sugar to avoid greeting your guests with telltale breath.

• **When a Recipe Calls for Garlic *and* Ginger:** Work with the garlic first, and follow up with the ginger, as it will remove the garlic smell from your hands, utensils, and cutting board.

• **To Remove the Smell from Hands:** Pretend a piece of silver-ware (it doesn't have to be real silver; stainless steel is fine) is a bar of soap and wash your hands with it under cold water.

Rub celery, tomato, or lemon on your hands.

GELATIN

• **To Keep Firm Longer:** When preparing anything made of gelatin, add one teaspoon white vinegar for four cups of liquid to postpone mold meltdown.

GINGER

• **To Preserve:** Fresh ginger root should be in every kitchen for medicinal purposes as well as for cooking. It can stay forever if it's re-frigerated in sherry and sealed in a covered jar. The ginger will not taste of sherry; the sherry will, however, acquire a gingery taste that's good to drink or to cook with.

GRAPES

• **Frozen Garnish:** Freeze bunches of grapes, and, for a party, add them to the punch bowl. They will not only look good in a bacchana-lian sort of way, but they'll also keep the punch cold. (For more unique tips on keeping liquids cold, see ICE CUBES below.)

• **Frozen Snack:** On a hot summer day . . . "Peel me a *frozen* grape, Beulah." Even with the peel still on, sucking on frozen grapes—one at a time—is a cooling, low-calorie treat.

GRAVY

• **To Get the Fat Out:** Put the gravy in a container and put the con-tainer in the freezer for about a half hour, until there's a solid layer of fat on top. Then spoon off that layer.

If you don't have time to freeze the gravy, remove the fat that's floating on top by blotting it up with a dry piece of bread.

• **The Taste of Wine:** When you add wine to gravy for taste, cook it for about ten minutes more than usual and you'll boil off the alcohol, but not the flavor of the wine.

HERBS

• **To Freeze Fresh Herbs:** Wash and cut them into pieces that will fit in ice-cube-tray compartments. Once the tray is filled with the pieces of herbs, add water to each compartment and let it freeze. Then transfer the cubes from the tray to plastic freezer bags. Don't forget to make note of which herbs you froze. When you want one for a recipe, take out a cube and either thaw it out or drop it in the pot.

• **When to Add Herbs:** For soup or stew, add *dried* herbs about one-half hour before the dish is done; add *fresh* herbs just ten minutes before you turn off the heat to help retain their color and flavor.

• **Dried Instead of Fresh or Fresh Instead of Dried:** When substituting *dried* herbs for *fresh* ones, use one-third of the amount called for in a recipe. For instance, if a recipe says one tablespoon fresh rosemary, use one teaspoon dried rosemary. Before adding the herbs, release their flavor by rolling them around in the palms of your hand so that they crumble. It goes without saying that to substitute *fresh* herbs for *dried* ones, use three times the amount of dried herbs the recipe calls for. Well, there, we've already said it.

• **To Microwave:** The flavor of dried herbs is heightened in the microwave, so go easy when using them. On the other hand, since fresh herbs are milder in the microwave, consider increasing the amount you use, if the recipe is not written specifically for microwave cooking.

• **Herb Vinegar** (See VINEGAR below.)

HONEY

• **To Reliquefy:** When a jar of honey crystallizes, fill a bowl with very hot water and put the jar in the bowl. After about five minutes, stir the honey, and keep stirring until it's reliquefied.

With the lid of the honey jar on, zap it in the microwave on *high* for about thirty seconds; fifteen seconds if there's not much honey; sixty seconds if it's a large, full jar.

ICE CUBES

• **Decorative Cubes:** Before freezing a tray of water, in each compartment put a twist of lemon or lime, a cherry, or a sprig of mint. Keep in mind the drinks you'll be serving and coordinate ice-cube trimmings. Ice cubes with edible flowers in water glasses . . . now that's a lovely idea.

• **To Prevent Diluting with Ice:** Make ice cubes out of the drinks you're serving. Have lemonade ice cubes for lemonade, punch ice cubes for punch, and . . . well, you've got the picture.

LEMONS AND LIMES

• **Just a Little Juice:** Don't dry out a whole lemon or lime by cutting it when all you need is a squirt or two of the juice. Instead, puncture the peel with the tip of a pointy knife and squeeze out whatever you need. Then close the opening with a piece of masking tape or cover the fruit with plastic wrap.

• **To Get the Most Juice:** Before squeezing, let the lemon or lime sit in hot water for five minutes, and/or roll the fruit around on a counter for a minute. When the inner membranes get broken down—and they will—the fruit will yield close to twice as much juice.

MARSHMALLOWS

• **To Soften:** Put hardened marshmallows in a plastic bag, along with a couple of slices of very fresh bread, and keep the bag closed for two or three days.

• **Pumpkin Pie Topping:** Layer the bottom of a crust with marshmallows, then pour the pumpkin pie filling on top of it. Bake as usual, but don't be surprised when the marshmallows make their way to the pie's surface to form a tufted topping.

MEAT

• **Salting a Roast:** When you make a roast, do you salt it? If you do, next time try salting it right before it finishes cooking. That way, the salt doesn't have a chance to draw out and absorb a lot of the meat's moisture and the roast will be a lot juicier.

• **To Reheat:** Wash two or three lettuce leaves and put them on a generous piece of aluminum foil, then put the meat on top of the leaves. Pinch the foil closed and reheat in a 350-degree oven. The lettuce will moisturize the meat as it reheats.

• **To Prevent Freezer Burn:** Wrap meat in two thick plastic food-storage bags, and before sealing, make it as airtight as possible. (See PLASTIC BAGS in Chapter 10, "Kitchen Stuff," for an easy way to make bags air-free.) That way it will not absorb any unwanted flavors from the freezer.

• **Thawing Meat:** Meat might thaw too slowly on a shelf in the refrigerator, too quickly on your kitchen counter. It will thaw thoroughly *and* stay cool, however, in an insulated container. Next time, use a Styrofoam chest for thawing meat, especially if you're out of the house all day.

• **Thawed Meat:** The process of *freezing* does not kill off all bacteria. Bacteria reactivate when food thaws. Use meat immediately after thawing to prevent spoilage.

• **Meatloaf:** If you're not a "hands on" kind of cook, take the yuck out of meatloaf making by putting the ingredients in a large, plastic, Ziploc bag. Zip it closed, then mush them all together from the outside of the bag.

• **Meatball Fillers:** Surprise your guests with unusual meatballs. Start with little chunks of cheese as the centers of the meatballs, then pack the meat around. Or use sautéed mushrooms, small pitted olives, halves of dried apricots, and so on. Use your own creative ideas, especially when you're serving them as hors d'oeuvres.

• **Hamburger Patties:** Talk about fast food. . . . Hamburgers will be done in less time than usual if you poke holes in the middle of the patties before broiling or grilling. (This is the secret behind the quick preparation of White Castle burgers.)

• **Meat Substitutes:** For those of you who want to cut down on fat, cooked bulgur or TVP, texturized vegetable protein (both are available at health-food stores and many supermarkets) can be used in place of ground beef in many dishes, such as chili, lasagna, ravioli, meat sauce, and sloppy joes.

MEAT TENDERIZER

• **MSG, Also Known as . . . :** There are ingredients composed mostly of the flavor enhancer monosodium glutamate that the Food and Drug Administration does not require manufacturers to list on packaging. If MSG does not agree with you, take note of the following ingredients on labels. They'll tip you off about the presence of MSG: hydrolyzed vegetable protein, hydrolyzed plant protein, and "natural flavoring or seasoning."

• **MSG Substitute:** Papaya is rich in papain, an enzyme that will help tenderize meat. Let the meat sit in papaya juice in the refrigerator for a few hours. Then blot the meat dry and prepare as usual.

An ounce or two of strong prepared tea added to a roast or stew will also help tenderize meat and cut down on cooking time.

MILK

• **To Prevent Boiling Over:** Put a clean stone or marble in the pot with the milk.

• **To Prevent Sticking:** Right before you put milk in a pot to heat it, rinse the pot with cold water.

• **When Milk Scorches:** Put the pot with the scorched milk in cold water and add a pinch of salt to the milk. This remedy will take away the milk's burnt taste.

• **Milk Substitutes:** For 1 cup whole milk for baking or cooking, use either 1 cup skim milk and 2 tablespoons melted (unsalted) butter or margarine, ½ cup evaporated whole milk and ½ cup water, or ¼ cup dry whole milk and ⅞ cup water.

MUFFINS

• **When They're Stuck to the Pans on the Bottom:** Wet a towel and spread it out on a counter. Let the hot muffin tin sit on the wet towel for a minute or two. You should then be able to pry the muffins out of the tin. Next time, bake them in paper baking cups.

• **For Lighter Muffins:** When the recipe calls for milk, substitute yogurt plus ½ teaspoon baking soda or buttermilk plus ½ teaspoon baking soda for each cup of milk called for in the recipe. Bet you'll like the consistency of the muffins better when you use the milk substitute.

• **Instant Frosting:** A few minutes before the muffins are done, place a marshmallow on top of each muffin. After the marshmallow meltdown, the muffins will come out frosted.

• **Fat Substitute** (See CAKE above.)

NUTS

• **Shelling Brazil Nuts:** When you're faced with tough nuts to crack, like Brazil nuts, keep them in the freezer and you'll have an easier time.

Folk Belief: Nuts!

♦

Eat a few pecans when you're looking for a job, and the search should

prove successful. (Be sure to brush your teeth before you go in for

that interview, though!)

♦

Eat three almonds right before going to sleep, and your dreams will be

in full color and vivid enough to remember.

• **Shelling Walnuts:** Let them soak overnight in salted water. Next morning, get out the nutcracker. The walnuts will open more easily and without crumbling.

• **Shelling Pecans:** Soaking pecans in just-boiled water for about ten minutes makes shelling a cinch.

• **Skinning Almonds:** Put shelled almonds in a strainer and plunk the strainer in a pot of just-boiled water. After a minute or two, take the almonds out of the water, let them cool off, and pinch the lower portion of each almond. The nut should slip right out of its skin.

ONIONS

• **To Prevent Tears:** Wear goggles or a scuba mask to protect your eyes.

Since cold slows down the movement of the pungent bulb's volatile molecules, onions that have been in the freezer for fifteen minutes or in the fridge for an hour will be kinder to your eyes.

Work with the onion under cold running water, or fill the sink or a basin with water and work with the onion while it's submerged.

• **To Keep Longer:** Cut an onion from the top down. If you work your way toward the root end, the onion will stay good longer, especially if you refrigerate the unused portion in a glass jar with the skin intact.

• **From Strong to Mild:** Slice a strong yellow onion in thin slices and place them in a bowl. Pour boiling water over them, let them stand for about two to three minutes, then drain and refrigerate until the slices are cold. You'll probably be surprised at how much they taste like a sweet Spanish onion.

• **When Onions Sprout:** If it's springtime, plant the sprouting onions in your garden. All other times of year, plant them in a flowerpot and place them in a sunny window. Use the growing green stalks the same way you would use scallions.

• **To Store:** Allow the air to circulate around onions by keeping them in an old—but clean—pantyhose leg (one more reason to save unwearable pantyhose).

• **Onion Substitutes:** When a recipe calls for one medium onion, you can use one tablespoon onion powder or one tablespoon instant minced onion.

PANCAKES

• **For Light, Fluffy Pancakes:** You've seen the commercials in which pancakes float off the plate, haven't you? Here's the secret: Replace the milk or any other liquid in the recipe with room-temperature club soda. But use the entire batter as soon as you make it—it won't keep.

PARSLEY

• **To Perk Up Parsley:** Cut off ½ inch from the stems, then put the wilted parsley in a glass of ice-cold water and refrigerate for at least an hour.
• **Natural Breath Deodorizer:** Use fresh sprigs of parsley as a garnish for garlicky and other spicy foods. The hard part is getting your guests to eat the parsley to clean their breath. If you find a way, please let us know.

PASTA

• **To Prevent Sticking:** Add one tablespoon vegetable oil to the water and the pasta won't stick together. Some cooks believe that as

Folk Belief: Pancake Mania

In England, Shrove Tuesday (the day before Ash Wednesday) is known

as Pancake Day. Eat a pancake on that day, and you'll have

a year filled with food, money, and luck.

the pasta cools the starch causes the stickiness, so if you keep the pasta warm try draining in a warmed colander and serving in a heated bowl, it won't clump up.

• **To Prevent Boiling Over:** Spread olive or vegetable oil an inch or two around the top inside of the pot, and the water won't boil over as much.

Spray nonstick vegetable spray on the inside of the top of the pot to help prevent boilover.

PEANUT BUTTER

• **For Freshness:** Store peanut butter upside down in the refrigerator to keep it fresher longer.

PEARS

• **To Core in Quantity:** Slice each pear in half and use a melon baller to scoop out the inedible center. It's quick, easy, and efficient.

PEAS

• **To Cook:** When you buy fresh peas in their pods, wash the pods and cook them in a pot of boiling water. When the peas are ready, the pods will pop to the top and can be shelled and served.

PIES

• **To Lock the Juice In:** Stand a four-inch piece of uncooked macaroni in the middle of the pie to prevent the juice from oozing out and making a mess in the oven.

• **For a Crisp Piecrust:** Use one tablespoon white vinegar in place of one tablespoon ice water called for in the recipe.

• **For a Flaky Piecrust:** Use sour cream or yogurt in place of the liquid called for in the recipe.

Before baking, dip a pastry brush in cold water and lightly stroke the crust with it.

Folk Belief: Piecrust

After you finish trimming a piecrust, think back. If you trimmed the crust

without changing hands (holding the pie plate or tin in one hand

while trimming with the other), you will have great wealth. It only

counts, however, if you don't do it that way on purpose.

PIMIENTOS

• **To Store:** Once you've opened a jar of pimientos, pour white vinegar in and refrigerate them; they will keep longer than you thought they would. If they taste a bit vinegary, rinse them with cold water before using.

PINEAPPLE

• **Selection:** Choose ripe pineapples, because once they're off the plant, they're not going to ripen anymore.
• **To Store:** Cut slices as you need them from the bottom of the pineapple, and cover the rest with plastic wrap. If you keep the leaves on, the fruit will stay fresh longer.

POPCORN

• **Bigger and Better:** For best results, sprinkle a little warm water on the kernels an hour before popping. Or keep your popping corn in the freezer, and you'll get fluffy popcorn with hardly any unpopped kernels.
• **If You Use a Hot-Air Popcorn Maker:** *Preheat it* and you will reap the rewards—larger, fluffier popcorn—and very few duds.

POTATOES

• **Keep the Skin On:** Don't peel potatoes before you boil them. Their skins keep the flavor and the nourishing ingredients from escaping. Once the potatoes are boiled, the skins will come off easily.

• **To Keep White Potatoes White:** If you're ignoring our advice to keep the skin on (above) when you boil white potatoes, add lemon juice or vinegar—one teaspoon to one pound of potatoes—and the potatoes will stay white.

• **To Store:** Put gingerroot with potatoes and both will both stay fresh longer.

• **To Bake Potatoes in Half the Time:** Bring them to a boil, turn off the heat, let them sit for fifteen minutes, then bake.

Potatoes will bake faster standing up in muffin tins. Be sure to fill the empty muffin cups with water.

Take a tenpenny nail (it's a three-inch-long nail that got its name because that's what it used to cost per hundred) and clean it thoroughly, then hammer it into the middle of the potato from end to end. The nail will help bake the potato from the inside out.

• **When Potatoes Sprout or Are Greenish:** It means that they've been exposed to light too long. It also means that they will taste bitter because of a poisonous alkaloid called solanine. Don't panic! We're not talking high levels of solanine, but enough so that you should not eat those sprouting, greenish potatoes.

RICE

• **Creative Boiling:** Prepare rice without water. Instead, use low-fat chicken or onion soup or vegetable or beef broth. If you're willing to experiment, try tomato juice, or come up with your own liquid substitute that goes well with rice.

• **To Keep White Rice White:** For each quart of water used to boil white rice, add one teaspoon lemon juice to the pot. The rice will be nice and white, and the grains won't clump together.

• **To Make Mock Saffron Rice:** As a substitute for saffron, the world's most expensive spice, use ½ teaspoon turmeric and ¼ teaspoon garlic powder for 2 cups uncooked rice. Prepare the rice as

Folk Belief: Hot Rice

After rice is cooked, if a ring has formed around the inside edge

of the pot, the pot's owner will become rich.

usual. It will be the orange-yellow color of saffron and similar in taste.

SALAD

• **To Toss a Salad:** An efficient way to toss a salad is to put it in a big plastic bag, hold the top closed, and do cartwheels. (Just kidding.) All you have to do is shake-shake-shake the bag. Instead of putting it in a big salad bowl, consider serving individual salad bowls to make it easy on your guests.

• **To Prevent Soggy Salads:** When preparing a salad in advance, put a saucer or larger dish (depending on the size of the salad bowl) facedown on the bottom of the bowl, then fill it with salad on top. That way, the salad won't sit in the water that drains off the just-washed veggies.

Folk Belief: Lettuce Be Rich

To attract money, eat a salad with lots of lettuce, along with

other salad greens and fresh dill.

SALT

• **Oops!—It's Too Salty:** When soup or stew or a sauce has been oversalted, this spud's for you. Take a peeled raw potato, cut it into half-a-dozen pieces, put them in the pot, and let them simmer for about ten minutes. By then they will have started to get soft *and* absorbed the salt.

Sugar and white vinegar can also help neutralize an oversalted dish. Gradually add them in the following proportions: ½ teaspoon sugar and ½ teaspoon vinegar. Taste and add, taste and add until the dish is just right.

• **To Prevent Oversalting:** Add salt right after the dish is prepared. By tasting the completed dish, you will be able to take into account the ingredients' natural sodium when determining how much salt is still needed. Chances are, you'll end up using less salt.

• **For a Free-Flowing Saltshaker:** Keep in the shaker some grains of rice—about ten grains in an average-size shaker—to absorb moisture and prevent salt grains from clumping up, especially in humid weather.

• **Shaking Less Salt:** If you're trying to cut down on your salt intake, you should have more control over the amount of salt that flows

❧

Folk Belief: Worth Your Salt

"Taking salt together" was an ancient good ol' boys bonding experience.

"There is salt between us" is a Middle Eastern expression denoting brotherhood. How about some salt for sisterhood? The Aztecs had a salt goddess.

Well, that counts for something.

Meanwhile, when you move into a new house, it's good luck to bring new salt with you, and leave the old box behind.

from your shaker. To do that, wash and dry the top of the shaker. Then, with colorless nail polish, paint over some of the holes on the inside of the shaker top. (Of course, the more holes you close up with the polish, the less salt will spill out.) Be sure that the polish is thoroughly dry before putting the top back on the shaker.

• **Salt and Foil:** Keep foods with a high salt content away from aluminum foil. Foil will rust when it comes into contact with salt—and no one wants to eat rusty food.

SANDWICHES

• **For Neat Sandwiches:** Make a pocket out of a bun to hold a usually messy sandwich filling. To do that you have to start with an unsliced bun. Cut off about an inch across the top. Then carefully scoop out the insides of the rest of the bun, forming the pocket. Spoon in the filling—sloppy joe, corned beef and potato salad, roast beef and cole slaw—and top it off with the top of the bun. This bun pocket will stop the filling from squishing out into your hands, on your lap, all over the table.

Of course, you can forget the bun entirely and just use pita bread.

• **To Prevent Sogginess:** Since it's usually mustard, ketchup, mayonnaise, or some kind of dressing that makes sandwich bread soggy, don't put it on the bread. Instead, smear it on whatever is in the middle of the sandwich, like meat or cheese. Also, if the sandwich is not going to be eaten as soon as it's prepared, wrap the wet things—lettuce, tomato, pickles, cucumber—separately, and assemble the sandwich right before eating it.

SAUSAGES

• **To Keep Them Intact:** Jab sausages with a fork before and while cooking them to prevent them from bursting out of their skins.

SHRIMP

• **For Flavor:** The tastiest ways to prepare shrimp are either to cook them with their shells on or—if they're already shelled—to simmer them in beer.

SOUP

• **Oversalted Soup** (See SALT above.)

• **To Remove Fat:** Refrigerate the soup and the fat will form a top-side layer that can then be scraped off with a spoon.

If you have broth that's fatty, pour it through a paper coffee filter.

After soup is taken off the fire, lay a leaf or two of lettuce on the soup's surface. Within a couple of minutes, when the leaves are coated with fat, remove them and throw them away.

There are basters readily available at housewares stores that separate fat from nonfat liquid. They're excellent for helping remove the top layer of fat from soup or gravy. (For more suggestions see GRAVY above.)

• **Soup Thickener:** Instead of the old standard thickeners, cornstarch and flour, you can use more interesting ingredients that won't add lumps or clumps. Mashed potatoes or instant potato flakes, for instance, crustless bread crumbs, quick-cooking oatmeal, or leftover cooked oatmeal. Whatever you choose, mix in only one tablespoon at a time and give it a minute, then check the consistency before adding more.

SOUR CREAM

• **To Substitute:** Use 1 cup cottage cheese, 1 teaspoon white vinegar, and ¼ cup skim milk in place of 1 cup sour cream.

In a pinch, use plain yogurt as a sour cream substitute.

SPAGHETTI

• **No More Puddle in the Plate:** If you wait until the spaghetti stops steaming before serving, you'll be rid of the water that makes a puddle on the plate when the steam condenses.

SPICES

• **To Store:** Keep spices in airtight containers away from the stove, in a cool, darkish place.

Most spices will keep their flavor longer if they're in the freezer.

• **When to Replace:** Since spices lose their kick after a while—anywhere from six months to a year—keep tabs by putting a date on each spice container the first time you open it. Unless you use enormous quantities of one or more spices, it's a good idea to buy the smallest sizes available.

• **Cooking with Inedible Spices:** Put inedible spices (such as bay leaves, whole cloves) in a metal tea ball or in a piece of cheesecloth tied with string, and immerse them in your soup or stew. When the dish is done, simply lift out the container of spice and discard it.

SUGAR

• **Other Words for Sugar:** When reading a label, if you don't see "sugar" on the list of ingredients, it doesn't mean there's no sugar in the product. Sugar may also be listed as dextrose, fructose, lactose, maltose, or sucrose. And even if none of the above are listed, it *still* doesn't mean the product is sugar-free—not if it contains corn syrup, honey, maple syrup, or molasses.

• **To Prevent White Sugar from Lumping:** Keep a couple of saltine crackers in the container.

• **For Hardened Brown Sugar:** Take your choice: Place the sugar in a jar with either a couple of marshmallows, a few slices of apple, a wedge of lemon or orange, or a slice of fresh bread. Make sure the lid on the jar is tightly closed. Allow a day or two for the sugar to unclump.

• **To Prevent Brown Sugar from Hardening:** Keep it in the freezer.

Folk Belief: Sugar 'n' Salt

If you stir in sugar instead of salt or salt instead of sugar, your dish may

not come out very tasty, but you will soon receive good news.

Keep brown sugar in a jar with a few prunes. The sugar will stay loose and the prunes, when you eat them, will be delicious.

• **To Substitute:** Instead of one cup brown sugar, use one cup white sugar and two tablespoons molasses.

In baking, if you use one cup of *brown* sugar in place of one cup *white* sugar, the end result may be a little moister and have a faint butterscotch taste.

SWEET CREAM

• **To Prevent Souring:** If you really need to use sweet cream that's just starting to sour, add a pinch of baking soda to bring back the sweetness. And use it . . . *now*!

TOMATOES

• **To Ripen:** Place green tomatoes in a plastic or paper bag with some apples and keep them in a cool, dark place. The apples give off an ethylene gas that will help ripen tomatoes more quickly than if they were left alone.

• **The Best Way to Slice 'Em:** To avoid cutting through a tomato's ovary walls, causing the pulp and juice to squish out, slice the fruit (yes, fruit) lengthwise, meaning vertically or up and down. The slices will stay firmer, keeping your sandwiches dryer and preventing the tomato juice from diluting your salad dressing.

• **Easy Peeling:** Dunk fresh tomatoes into just-boiled water for about thirty seconds, then into cold water for another thirty seconds. This will cause the skins to crack, making them easy to peel off.

TOMATO SAUCE

• **To Sweeten Sauce:** Grate in some carrots. They do the job as well as sugar and are a lot more nutritious.

Folk Belief: Tomatoes Aren't Just Tasty

In some Italian homes, a big, beautiful, red tomato sits on the mantel

to attract prosperity, while in others, the inhabitants subscribe to the

belief that eating tomato sauce brings health and wealth.

TURKEY

• **A Gauge for Stuffing:** Figure ½ cup stuffing per pound of un-cooked weight.
• **To Remove Stuffing Easily:** Put the stuffing in cheesecloth, then insert it into the turkey. When the turkey is done, you can remove the stuffing by simply pulling out the cheesecloth.
• **Nonstick Roasting:** Line the bottom of the roasting pan with cleaned celery stalks and lay the turkey on top of it. The celery acts as a roasting rack, allowing the gravy to drain to the bottom of the pan. When the turkey is done cooking, it won't be stuck to the bottom of the pan. After taking out the bird, just throw away the celery.
• **Basting:** Consider getting a baster that separates the fat from the juice (available at housewares stores). Baste with the juice; discard the fat.
• **To Know When It's Done:** In addition to watching for that little button that pops up, jab the turkey thigh with a fork. The bird is done if the juice that seeps out is clear.

TURNIPS

• **To Lessen Their Smell:** Add a teaspoon of sugar to the water while cooking turnips, and that unpleasant smell will practically disappear. Okay, it won't be half as bad. Well, it'll be a lot more tolerable.

VEGETABLES

• **To Store Root Veggies:** Cut off the leafy tops or they'll rob the roots (the part you eat) of nutrients.

Line the vegetable bin with paper towels, or keep a dry sponge there to help absorb moisture. The less moisture there is, the longer the veggies will stay fresh.

• **To Remove Pesticides:** Jay Kordich, known as "the Juiceman," shared his method of removing poisonous sprays from produce. Fill the sink or a basin with cold water and add four tablespoons salt and the fresh juice of half a lemon. This makes a diluted form of hydrochloric acid. Soak most fruits and vegetables five to ten minutes; leafy greens two to three minutes; berries—including strawberries—one to two minutes. After soaking, complete the process by rinsing thoroughly in cold water.

An alternative to the Juiceman's method is to soak produce in a sink or basin filled with water and ¼ cup white vinegar. Then scrub appropriate produce with a vegetable brush under cold water. Give it a final rinse, and it's ready to be used.

• **To Revive Wilting Greens:** Put the droopy greens in ice water with a couple of tablespoons of lemon juice. Then cover them and put them in the fridge. After about an hour, they should be perked up.

• **To Stir-Fry:** The secret to stir-frying all vegetables evenly is to cut them all the same size. To prevent them from sticking, heat up the wok before adding the oil.

VINEGAR

• **To Make Herb Vinegar:** The measurements are about one heaping tablespoon fresh herbs to about one pint white-wine vinegar. Sterilize a jar by pouring just-boiled water in it and be sure it has a rustproof screw-on lid. Of course, if the vinegar is going to be a gift, you'll want to select an *attractive* jar. You'll also need a funnel and the herb of your choice (rosemary, chives, basil, tarragon, or sweet marjoram—each works well). Wash and dry the fresh herb and place it in the jar. Heat the vinegar, stopping right before it begins to boil. With the help of the funnel, pour the vinegar into the jar, screw the lid on tight, and let it steep for a couple of weeks in a cool, dark place. Then either strain out the herb or don't, depending on whether you like the way the herb looks in the jar. Just keep in mind, the longer the herb stays in, the stronger the lingering flavor. Don't forget to label the jar and set its expiration date for six months hence.

• **Warning:** *Do not* use painted plates to serve food that has vinegar in it (e.g., salad with vinaigrette dressing). The vinegar will eat into the paint and leach out the lead, which can prove dangerously toxic. If you have any question about the plates you use, buy a lead-testing kit and check them out.

WATER

• **When You're Out of Filtered Water:** Add ½ pinch of vitamin C powder or a tiny piece of vitamin C tablet to the water right before you drink it. A chemical reaction that takes place between the chlorine and the acidic vitamin makes the unwanted taste and smell of chlorine in tapwater disappear.

WATERMELON

• **For a Picnic:** When you're ready to leave for the picnic grounds, take the watermelon out of the refrigerator and wrap it in dry newspaper. When you're ready to eat the melon, unwrap it for a cool, fresh-tasting treat.

• **Fruit Pops:** Remove the seeds from a big chunk of watermelon, then purée the melon in the blender. Pour the puréed pulp into children's Popsicle makers or ice-cube trays, then put them in the freezer. The results are a delicious natural treat for hot weather.

WHIPPED CREAM

• **What It Takes:** It takes one cup heavy or whipping cream to make two cups whipped cream.

• **To Get the Job Done More Quickly:** Add ¼ teaspoon lemon juice or a pinch of salt to whoop that heavy whipping cream into whipped cream.

WINE

- **To Store:** Since wine bottles should be kept on their sides so that the corks stay wet, your best bet is a wine rack.
- **Dripless Pouring:** Just as you finish pouring the wine and are about to lift it away from the glass, give the bottle a subtle twist, and the drip will dissipate as it rolls around the bottle's lip.
- **To Serve Red Wine:** It is said that red wine should be served at "room temperature." When that standard was set, room temperature meant 65 degrees. Nowadays, the average home is a warmer 68–72 degrees, but red wine should still be served at about 60–65 degrees.
- **The Amount to Serve:** The wine drinker wants room in the glass to swirl the wine and bring out its full bouquet. Therefore, use a large wine glass and fill it no more than one-third to one-half full.
- **When Not to Serve Wine:** When you're serving pickled food, salad with a vinegar dressing, or other dishes that are vinegary, your guests' palate will be numbed to the taste of wine.

Folk Belief: Pass the Wine

Always pass a bottle of wine around a table clockwise. If you pass it around

counterclockwise, legend has it that it will turn to vinegar.

12

KID STUFF

ARTWORK

• **To Prevent Smudging:** Lightly zap a drawing—chalk, pencil, crayon, or watercolors—with hair spray, and it will protect the picture from smudging and fading.

BABY FOOD

• **Do-It-Yourself Baby Food:** If available, use organic fruits and vegetables. Steam them or put them in the microwave (a method that is said to retain more of the nutrients), then purée them. To prepare food in advance, fill ice-cube trays with the puréed vegetables or fruit and cover with aluminum foil. Once the food is frozen, put the cubes in freezer bags. Don't forget to label and date them. Two average cubes are about a three-ounce serving. (If you do not normally use organic produce, see TO REMOVE PESTICIDES in Chapter 11, "Food," under VEGETABLES.)

• **To Prevent Cross-Contamination:** If your baby does not routinely finish the contents of an entire jar at one feeding, do not feed him directly from the jar. Think about it. The spoon goes into the baby's mouth, then into the jar, contaminating the contents. When you put the jar away, bacteria have a chance to grow in that unused portion of food. Instead, put a portion in a dish and refrigerate the balance in the *uncontaminated* jar.

BAND-AIDS

• **To Remove Painlessly:** Soak a cotton ball with vegetable oil or baby oil and dab it all over the Band-Aid, then gently peel it off.

Let a hair dryer blow warm air on the Band-Aid for a minute or two. The heat will melt the sticky stuff, making it possible to peel without pain.

BATH TIME

• **To Get a Grip:** A baby is slippery when wet and sudsy. Wear soft cotton gloves when bathing a baby. It's also a good idea to line the bathing area—tub or sink—with a large, soft towel.

• **Small Baby/Big Bathtub:** When the baby has just outgrown the sink, make the tub smaller and the bathing process safer by putting a clean, hard-plastic lattice-type clothes basket in the tub in which to bathe the baby.

• **To Keep Dry:** Cover your front with a big towel, keeping it in place with a spring-type clothespin behind your neck. The towel will keep you dry and be handy to dry the baby when you've finished bathing her.

BOTTLE

• **To Keep a Bottle Warm for Late-Night or Outdoor Feeding:** As you warm your baby's bottle, put hot water in a wide mouthed thermos. When the baby's bottle is just the right temperature, pour the water out of the thermos and replace it with the baby's bottle. Put the lid on the thermos, and the bottle will be ready when you're away from home or in the middle of the night.

• **To Clean Out Chalky Deposits:** Boil bottles in one quart water and two cups white vinegar for about fifteen minutes. Rinse thoroughly and sterilize as usual.

• **To Get Rid of Milk or Juice Smell:** Put three heaping tablespoons baking soda in a pot with a quart of water and the smelly bottles. Bring the pot to a boil and let it boil for a couple of minutes. Rinse and sterilize as usual.

• **When Plastic Bottles Leak Away From Home:** Take off the cap and nipple, put a piece of plastic wrap over the bottle's opening, then screw the cap and nipple back on. (Of course, you realize that, while the bottle won't leak, you won't be able to feed the baby this way.)

• **To Help Wean a Child Off the Bottle:** Fill a cup with baby's favorite drink. Fill the bottle with something that's healthful but not as delicious. Let him taste both and see which one he selects.

BUBBLES

• **Make Your Own Solution:** If your kids are forever blowing bubbles, it's a lot more economical to whip up a batch of the sudsy solution whenever it's needed. Combine one tablespoon powdered detergent with one tablespoon glycerine, one cup just-boiled water, and a few drops food coloring. Stir until the powder completely dissolves. Store it in a jar with a screw-on lid.

• **Make Your Own Bubble Blower:** You can use a plastic straw to blow bubbles simply by cutting the end diagonally.

• **To Make Humongous Bubbles:** Take a plain wire hanger and reshape it so that it becomes a large round hoop with a handle. Pour the bubble solution into a pan or cookie sheet that's at least a little wider than the hoop. Now you or your child can dunk the hoop in the goop and wave it through the air at just the right speed (not too fast, not too slow) to make a big, beautiful bubble.

CHOICES

• **Stack the Odds in Your Favor:** When you want your child to choose to do something, eat something, go someplace, or wear something, mention *your* preference last and, chances are, the last one mentioned will be the child's first choice.

CLAY (PLAY-DOUGH)

While testing many different formulas, we acquired enough clay to sculpt the Venus de Milo *with* arms. These are the two recipes that will produce the best clay simply and inexpensively:

• **To Knead into Clay:** In a plastic container, combine one cup salt and two cups flour, then gradually add water until it's the consistency of workable clay. Store it in an airtight container.

• **To Make Cooked Clay:** In a saucepan, mix 2 cups baking soda (2 cups baking soda equals 1 one-pound box) with 1 cup cornstarch, then add 1¼ cups cold water. (Food coloring is optional.) Cook the mixture over a medium flame, stirring-stirring-stirring. When it's the consistency of moist mashed potatoes, turn off the heat, dump it on a plate, and cover it with a damp cloth. When it's cool to the touch, it's ready. Store it in an airtight plastic bag or container in the refrigerator. Before using it, let it get to room temperature.

• **The Claying on of Hands:** There are all kinds of artsy craftsy things a child can do with clay, a little imagination, and tools from the kitchen, such as a cookie cutter. But of all the activities we've heard of, this is the project that made the best *impression* on us: Line a pie tin with about an inch of clay. Have your child spread his fingers and press down on the clay to make an impression of his hand. If you eventually want to hang it up, use a straw to cut out a hanging hole. Let the clay dry thoroughly (it may take a couple of days, unless you speed up the process by baking it in the oven on a low setting for about fifteen minutes). When you're sure it's dry, paint it with acrylics, watercolors, poster paints, or felt-tip markers. To protect it, add a coat of varnish, shellac, or colorless nail polish.

• **To Prepare the Sculptor:** Give your child's hand the once-over with a bar of dry soap (no water), and the waxy coating will make it easier for her to work with the clay.

CLOSETS

• **Within Reach:** Hang a pocket-style shoe bag in the child's closet low enough for him to keep whatever it is that he keeps—crayons, small toys, UFOs (unidentified found objects). It will teach him to be organized, and it gets stuff off the floor.

A pocket-style shoe bag hung in the closet is also wonderful for accessories, such as hats, scarves, mittens, galoshes, sunglasses, sunscreen, and easily accessible to your child.

CRAYON

• **To Clean a Blackboard:** Erase crayon marks without scratching the slate by massaging it with a paste of baking soda and water on a sponge or cloth.

CRIB

• **A Convenient Holder:** Attach a towel rack on the outside of the crib to hold an extra blanket, towel, or clothing. A bicycle basket attached on the outside end of the crib can also come in handy to hold odds and ends, such as powder, pins, diapers, and hair bands.

• **To Stop a Moving Crib:** If you have a wooden floor, chances are your baby will learn that by shaking the crib he can move it around the room. You can prevent this from happening by putting self-stick bunion pads under the feet of the crib. If that doesn't do the job, cut four pieces of a bathtub mat—the kind with little suction cups—and put them under the crib's feet.

DIAPERS

• **Washing Cloth Diapers:** During the last rinse cycle add one cup white vinegar to remove whatever you used in the wash (detergent, bleach) that may irritate baby's sensitive skin.

• **Diaper Pail Deodorant:** Before lining the pail with a plastic bag, sprinkle in some baking soda. Each time you throw in a diaper, pour in some baking soda. When you empty the pail, wash it out with baking soda.

FOODS THAT DRIP

• **Ice-Cream Cones:** When you prepare an ice-cream cone for a child, put a small glob of peanut butter in the bottom of the cone, then add the scoop or two of ice cream. The peanut butter will stop the melting ice cream from dripping out the bottom. When the child eats his way to the cone's end, he'll have peanut butter with ice cream—a surprise treat.

• **Frozen Ice Pops:** Create a drip shield by poking the stick of the pop through the middle of a plastic lid, a shallow plastic container, or a coffee filter. You and your carpet will be glad you did.

GAMES
(OR ANYTHING THAT COMES
WITH A PAGE OF INSTRUCTIONS)

• **How Not to Lose the Instructions:** As soon as your child gets anything with a page of instructions, tape the instructions to the inside cover of the box. Then pray that your child doesn't lose the cover of the box!

GARDENING
(See DIG IN CHILDREN, in
Chapter 14, "Gardening.")

GIFT WRAP

• **A Personal Baby Gift Wrap:** If a baby's birth was announced in the newspaper, save the page and wrap your gift with it, making sure the announcement is somewhere on top of the package, circled in pink or blue, and spritzed with hair spray for a glossy finish.
• **Juvenile Gift Wrap:** The comics section of the newspaper as gift wrap is not a novelty anymore, but it's colorful and fun to receive. Or if the child who will be receiving the gift is interested in a particular subject—computers, nature, clothes, movies—take out the appropriate newspaper page and use that as wrapping. Again, spritz with hair spray to give it a more finished look and feel.

HAIR

• **To Remove Chewing Gum:** Put a glob of smooth peanut butter on the gummed area and rub the gum and peanut butter between

your fingers, working the gum out of the hair. Use a comb to finish the job, then shampoo and rinse as usual.
• Egg white is an effective gum remover, if you don't mind the sliminess.
• **Painless Baby Shampooing:** Massage a little petroleum jelly around baby's eyes and eyebrows so that when you shampoo, the suds will run off to the sides rather than into her eyes.

Entice your toddler into wearing goggles for his next shampoo, and turn it into a tearless adventure.
• **To Prevent Barrettes from Slipping:** Glue a couple of strips of Velcro to the insides of the barrette and it will hold the hair in place.

HIGH CHAIR

• **To Keep Baby from Sliding Down:** Stick nonslip bathtub appliqués on the inside back and seat of the high chair. Or cut a bathtub mat to fit the seat.
• **To Keep High Chair from Overturning:** If you're using a hand-me-down high chair—an old wooden one that a superactive child can rock back and forth until it overturns—secure it to a wall. (This may be a job for a handy person.) Put two hooks on the back of the high chair and two eyes appropriately lined up in the wall. Put the hooks in the eyes and you'll have some peace of mind when your child is in the high chair.
• **A Convenient Holder:** Attach a paper-towel dispenser to the back of the high chair, so you can reach around and grab a paper towel for those frequent wipe-ups. If you have an old wooden high chair that's braced to the wall (see TO KEEP HIGH CHAIR FROM OVERTURNING above), attach the paper-towel dispenser under the high chair seat.

JACKETS

• **Outgrowing Overnight:** Doesn't it seem as though a kid's arms can grow a couple of inches in the middle of the night? If it's too late in the season to invest in new winter outerwear, lengthen the arms of the jacket by sewing on knitted cuffs (available at notion counters), or ribbed sock cuffs. Make the color of the sleeve extenders match the jacket, and you won't have to worry about the child's rebuffing the cuffing.

LUNCHBOX

• **To Prevent Mold:** Mix equal parts of white vinegar and water and sponge out a lunchbox at the same time you do the dinner dishes.

MATTRESS

• **Bedwetting:** Use paper towels to blot up as much moisture as possible from the wet mattress. Then pour baking soda on that area and leave it to thoroughly dry. Then vacuum up the baking soda.

MEDICINE

• **Make It More Palatable:** If your child has to take something terrible-tasting, have him suck on an ice cube for a minute to numb his taste buds. Even if this process isn't completely successful, he won't know it till after he's taken the medicine.

MITTENS

• **To Prevent Lost Mittens:** On the upper side of each mitten's cuff, sew on a button that's the same size as the buttons on the coat that your child wears. Then teach him to button the mittens to the coat's buttonholes each time he takes off his coat and mittens.

There's always the tried-and-true strand of wool crocheted to the cuff of one mitten, connected to a chain stitch long enough to go up the sleeve, across the shoulders, and down the other sleeve, then crocheted to the other mitten. When your child takes off her coat and the mittens just hang there, it makes a real fashion statement, namely, "These mittens will not get lost!"

MUFFIN TINS

• **Eating in Bed:** When your child is sick and has to eat his meals in bed, use a muffin tray with paper liners. You'll have more leverage and less spillage.

• **For Nonslide Serving:** When your child gets to that helpful stage and insists on distributing refreshments, let the butler-in-training carry cold drinks in a muffin tin to prevent a tray mishap. But remember, it's not advisable to carry *hot* drinks on a *metal* tray.

PARTY TIME

• **Invitations:** Blow up balloons and, with a marker, print the invitation on them. Then let out the air and mail them to the invited guests. You might want to tie a tag on the balloon that says something like "You're invited to blow up this balloon for another invitation."

• **Party Treats:** Don't throw away empty toilet-paper or paper-towel rolls. Each can be filled with candy and little gifts, then wrapped with tissue paper and tied at both ends with ribbon or yarn for a fun party favor. If your child is having a sit-down party, put a guest's name on each, and set the table using them as place cards. Helium-inflated balloons with names marked on also make great place-holders—just tie each to the appropriate chair.

• **Impromptu Little Birthday Candleholders:** Colorful, inexpensive, easy-to-get Life Savers or marshmallows make in-a-pinch, save-the-day candleholders.

PESTICIDES ON FRUITS AND VEGETABLES
(See VEGETABLES in Chapter 11, "Food.")

PICTURE-TAKING

• **To Get Unique Expressions:** Instead of *you* making faces to get the toddler to smile, put a piece of transparent tape on his finger, and—as he tries to peel it off—snap photos of the faces *he's* making.

Use your imagination and creativity for taking pictures of your child, either with a still camera or a camcorder. For instance, a piece of bubble wrap can elicit all kinds of reactions from a child. Or put transparent tape on the end of her nose and pull it up to her forehead, asking her to do an imitation of Babe or Miss Piggy. Of course, whatever fun things you decide to try, just make sure they're all safe.

PLAY-DOUGH
(See CLAY above.)

SAFETY

• **In Case of Fire:** Call your local fire department and ask about "tot finder" decals that let firemen know that a child lives on the premises. If the department doesn't have them, the representative should be able to tell you where to get them. If you live in an apartment, put the decal on the front door. If you live in a house, put it on the entrance door, on the windows of the nursery and child's room, and on the bottom of the door to the nursery and child's room.

• **Standing Out in a Crowd:** As soon as your child is walking and socializing and you can take him outdoors, dress him in bright clothes that you can spot in an instant.

• **Children *Should* Be Heard:** When going out, especially in crowds, tie a whistle around your child's neck and teach her to blow the whistle over and over if she gets separated from you.

• **A Bell of an Alarm System:** Attach bells to cabinet doors, closet doors, the backs of drawers, and all exit doors that are no-nos for toddlers. The second you hear a bell, you'll know to go running.

• **A Burning Fireplace:** *Never* burn colored newspapers or magazines in the fireplace. Colored paper contains toxins, including lead. When the paper burns, the lead becomes airborne and can be inhaled, which is very dangerous, especially for children.

• **Table Padding:** The pointed corners of tables are scary when you have a toddler running around. Tape unused shoulder pads on those corners. It may not look good, but it's only a temporary measure.

• **Piano Protection:** The part of the piano that covers the keyboard is called a *fallboard,* and it's easy to see why. To prevent the fallboard from snapping down on a toddler's fingers, glue a standing cork on each end of the keyboard.

• **Glass Screen Door Caution:** Place strips of colored tape across a glass or screen door at your child's eye level as a constant reminder to her that the door is closed and not to run through it.

SHOES

• **New Shoes:** Lightly sandpaper the soles of new shoes to make them less slippery.

• **To Clean White Baby Shoes:** Sprinkle baking soda on a damp cloth and wipe them clean. Rinse with a clean, damp cloth and buff them dry.

• **Knowing Right from Left:** Tape an "R" on the insole of the child's right shoe and an "L" on the left insole. Now all you have to do is to teach your child which foot is *right* and which is *left.*

• **Sneaker Odor Eaters:** Ah, another use for unwearable panty-hose. Cut them off at the knees. Fill both of the foot portions with kitty litter and put one in each sneaker. Keep them there overnight, and in the morning, when you empty out the sneakers, the odor should be gone.

• **To Clean Sneakers:** Wash with a wet scouring pad and soap, then wipe them off with a sponge dampened with lemon juice.

SHOELACES

• **To Keep Them Tied:** Dampen shoelaces, then tie them and they'll stay tied.

• **How to Determine Length:** Count the number of openings that the shoelace goes into on both sides of the shoe or sneaker. Multiply that number by three and you get the length—in inches—of the shoelace needed. So, when there are ten shoelace holes (10x3=30) you'll need a thirty-inch shoelace.

• (For more tips see SHOELACES in Chapter 6, "Laundering.")

Folk Belief: Wish Upon a Shoelace

Make a wish when you're lacing someone else's shoes, and you put the odds

in your favor of the wish coming true. (Heed the old warning:

Be careful what you wish for.)

TOYS, PLASTIC

• **To Clean Dolls and Other Hard Plastic Toys:** Make a paste by combining ¼ cup baking soda with 1 tablespoon liquid dish detergent. Dip a toothbrush in the paste and brush the dirt away, then wipe the doll with a clean, damp sponge.

TOYS, STUFFED

• **Weekly Deep Freeze:** A teddy bear and other cuddly creatures become home to dust mites. To kill those microscopic mites—which can trigger allergic reactions such as asthma attacks—simply put the stuffed toy in a plastic bag and leave it in the freezer for twenty-four hours once a week. Explain to your child that his stuffed toy joined the *Ice Capades* and must be "on ice" every Monday.
• **To Dry-Clean:** If a stuffed toy isn't machine washable, put it in a plastic bag and add ½ cup cornstarch or baking soda. Then close the bag and shake-shake-shake. Take the toy out of the bag over a sink and pat out the cornstarch or baking soda. Finish the job with a hairbrush or vacuum.
• **To Clean Vinyl Toys:** Wipe vinyl with baking soda on a damp sponge. Rinse and dry.

TRAVEL

• **Airplane Takeoff and Landing:** To make air travel more comfortable for baby's sensitive little ears, feed her a bottle of whatever she prefers to drink. The constant swallowing, especially during takeoff and landing, can help equalize ear pressure.

• **Car Safety:** To make sure that a car door *never* closes on your child's fingers, teach him to clap hands the second he gets in the car. If it takes a big "Hooray!" so be it. The important thing is that you will close the door *after* you hear him clapping, knowing his fingers are safe.

• **When Parents Travel:** Prepare a special (audio or video) taped message to leave for your child each time you travel without her. Tell her you love her and can't wait to be home with her soon. If there's a favorite story or song or poem, read, sing, or recite it. Hey, it's your child, we bet you know exactly what she'll want to hear from you.

13

PETS

CATS AND DOGS

FLEAS

• **Do-it-Yourself Flea Collar:** Some commercial flea collars and sprays contain very strong ingredients that can cause your pet physical problems. You can make an *herbal* flea collar by soaking a durable, comfortable leather strap or heavy-but-smooth twine in pennyroyal oil (available at health-food stores) for twenty-four hours. Then tie it around your pet's neck, and fleas will flee. *Caution:* Do *not* use pennyroyal if you or your pet is pregnant. In rare instances it has caused cats to abort.

• **Flea Repellents:** Fleas have a keen sense of smell. Assault their little noses by stuffing a small pillow with cedar chips or shavings and keeping it on or near your pet's bed.

Cut two lemons into bite-sized pieces and place them—peel and all—in a pan with a quart of water. Boil for an hour, take them off the burner, and let them steep overnight. Next morning, strain and use the liquid to sponge down or spray your pet. Fleas will be repelled by the smell of citrus oil. The lemon water will also help heal existing flea bites on your pet's skin.

Your pet's diet is said to play the most effective role in repelling fleas, specifically the addition of vitamin B_1 (thiamin) to the menu. Brewer's yeast (available at health-food stores) is a rich source of B_1 and highly recommended. Daily dosage: one rounded tablespoon for fifty pounds of pet. To prevent brewer's yeast from causing gas, feed it to your pet in small amounts in moist food. You may also want to rub some brewer's yeast on your pet's coat and even take a daily dose yourself to ward off those nasty fleas.

Spike your pet's drinking water with white vinegar, one teaspoon to one quart water.

Raw garlic can help prevent or get rid of fleas, worms, coughs, constipation, indigestion, and more. Mince fine one to three cloves of garlic (depending on your pet's size) and add it to his food. If your pet has a problem eating it, try garlic powder or garlic oil in his food.

• **Getting Rid of Fleas:** Fleas breed and hatch in carpeting and on furniture. (WARNING: The following remedy is gross, but it works.) Put on a pair of white socks and slowly walk through your home— across carpeting and in places your pet frequents. Fleas will be attracted to your body heat and electromagnetic energy and jump on your feet. They'll be easy to see on the white socks so you can vacuum them away using the attachment called the crevice tool.

To catch fleas without getting so *personally* involved, put water in a pie tin, *gently* add one tablespoon liquid dish detergent (try not to create bubbles), and set the bowl on the floor in the room where your pet hangs out. Then put a lamp with at least a sixty-watt bulb next to it, with the lamp shining on the bowl. Darken the room except for that light and leave it overnight. The plan is for fleas to jump at the light and fall in the dish. Next morning, flush away the floating fleas. Repeat the procedure again at night. Do it every night for two weeks to get all the fleas—including the ones not yet hatched at the beginning of the process.

FEEDING PETS

• **Canned Food:** When using the whole can, open each end and push out the food with one of the lids. It's easier and more efficient than scooping it out from one end.

• **Place Mat:** Serve your pet's food on a no-longer-used floor mat from a car or a bathtub mat. The bowl won't move around during dinner, and the mat is easy to clean.

• **A Stay-Put Dish:** Glue a rubber jar ring to the bottom of your pet's dish to keep it from moving.

• **Insect-Free Food:** Sprinkle baking soda around your pet's dish to keep insects away.

• **To Remove Pet-Food Smell in Fridge:** Put the opened cans of dog or cat food in empty coffee cans and close with the plastic lid. The food's freshness stays in the can while the food's smell stays out of the refrigerator.

• **Storing Dry Food:** To be sure that neighborhood critters will not gnaw their way through the dry food in paper bags that you've stored in the garage, put the bags of food in big plastic garbage cans with secure lids.

• **Antifreeze Alert:** Keep dogs and cats away from the little puddles of sweet syrup under or near a car. Most likely it's ethylene glycol, better known as antifreeze, and as palatable as it is, that's how harmful it is.

BEDDING

• **To Deodorize Cloth Bedding Between Washings:** Cover the bedding with a thin layer of baking soda. Leave it on for thirty minutes, then vacuum it up or beat it out over the bathtub.

COLLARS

• **Protection at Night:** Put reflector tape—available at hardware stores—on your pet's collar so she can be seen more easily in the dark.

• **Make a Collar:** Recycle a belt you no longer intend to wear. Cut it down to comfortably fit your pet's neck and punch a few holes. There you have it—a new collar.

LOST-PET PREPARATION

• **Easy ID:** Photograph your pet and keep the clear, well-lit picture and a complete description of him, including all of his markings, with your other important papers. If your pet gets lost, that photo and information may help others find him fast.

PLANTS

• **Positioning Plants:** Become aware of your pet's favorite hangouts. Keep in mind that cats are territorial animals and want their place in the sun. Do not block that place with a plant.

Dogs like to look out windows. Leave windows clear of obstructions to allow your dog his favorite views.

• **Protecting Plants:** To make sure your pet doesn't get at your potted plants, put a tablespoon of white vinegar in your mister and spray the plants. Or cover the soil with pebbles, wire mesh, seashells, or horticultural charcoal, marbles, or whatever else will hide the soil without harming the plants.

CATS

CAT CARE AND FEEDING

• **To Pick Up a Cat:** If you think you're supposed to pick up a cat by the nape of its neck, then you've seen too many cartoons. The proper way is with one hand on its belly, while the other hand provides support under its rump and hind feet.

• **Making Nice:** Pet a cat the way the fur lies. In other words, go with the grain. Stroking a cat in the opposite direction may rub him the wrong way.

• **Brushing Shorthaired Cats:** Do shorthaired cats a favor and brush where they can't reach themselves—between their shoulders.

Folk Belief: Cat Sneezes

If a cat sneezes once, a happy event can be expected.

• **Appetite Stimulator:** If your cat walks away from her food, make it more appealing by drizzling some oil from a can of tuna fish over it.

• **Pill Popping:** Get a good grip on your cat, either on your lap or between your knees. Next, open his mouth by putting pressure on each side of his jaw. Place the pill as far back on the tongue as possible. Then keep his mouth closed and gently massage his throat to make him swallow. You may want to do this when someone else is around to help you, just in case he starts getting ornery.

• **Liquid Medicine:** If you can't sneak the medicine into your cat's food, and she refuses to take it, let her instincts take over. Drip it on her fur where she can reach it, then watch her lick it up.

CATS—TRAINING

• **Keep Away From . . . :** Whenever your cat invades forbidden territory, spritz him with a water gun or plant mister. Before long, he'll get the message.

• **Off! Off!** To train a cat to stay off a particular piece of furniture, next time she is on it, dip a cotton ball in vinegar and touch her mouth with it. Then put the cotton on a piece of plastic on the furniture as a reminder.

Since cats are bothered by stickiness on their fur and whiskers (wouldn't you be?) tape several strips of tape, with sticky side out, across taboo surfaces. (The kitchen counter would be first on my strips-of-tape list.)

Folk Belief: Wedding Cat

Planning a wedding? Don't forget to include a cat on the invitation list.

When a feline friend sits in on the nuptials, the couple

will be blessed with bliss.

• **To Prevent Scratched Furniture:** Buy or make a scratching post by nailing a piece of leftover carpet to a board. Put a little catnip on the post to make it more appealing than the furniture your cat is scratching. If the post doesn't distract her from the furniture, rub hot chili sauce on the woodwork and buff it with a soft cloth. If you don't want to put sauce on the wood, then sprinkle cayenne pepper on strips of tape and, without damaging the furniture, tie, tuck, pin, clip, or clamp it to the side where the cat likes to scratch.

CAT'S LITTER BOX

• **To Deodorize:** Baking soda, of course. Layer the bottom of the litter box with it, then add litter—about one cup baking soda to three pounds litter.
• **To Prevent Infection:** Wear gloves when you clean the litter box. Better safe than toxoplasmosis, the parasitic disease that can be transmitted by cats' feces.

DOGS

DOG CARE AND FEEDING

• **Appetite Increaser:** If your dog is not eating and you're getting concerned, feed him some stale beer. It just may whet his appetite.
• **Pill Popping:** If your dog won't take a pill, push the pill into a chunk of something he likes but hardly ever gets, like peanut butter, cheese, or liver pâté.

Incidentally, never give dogs chocolate; it's bad for them. Dogs don't metabolize theobromine, an alkaloid found in chocolate. If eaten by a dog, a toxic dose—about .04 ounces of baker's chocolate or about .04 ounces of milk chocolate per kilogram body weight— may cause signs of chocolate poisoning. It can produce cardiac failure and be fatal.

• **Liquid Medicine:** If you know your dog is going to be uncooperative when it comes to taking medicine, put her in the bathtub. Let her stand on a rubber mat or towel. It's better to spill the liquid in the tub than on carpeting. Also, she can't run too far when stuck in the tub. Calm her down as much as possible. Pull out the corner of her lower lip so that a pocket is formed. Next, take the filled dropper and dispense the medicine into that pocket, a little at a time. Hold her jaws closed until she swallows. You may have to gently rub her throat to make her swallow. While this is an effective process, you may need someone else's help to control the squirming patient.

• **Bathing—to Prevent Clogged Drains:** Don't forget to put a "hair catcher" over the drain before each bath. They're inexpensive and available at hardware stores in two sizes. Be sure to measure the diameter of your bathtub's pop-up stopper. Or if you have to make do, put a small strainer over the stopper to prevent the dog's hair from going down the drain.

• **Bathing—for a Soft and Shiny Coat:** Add a few tablespoons baking soda to the wash and rinse water.

• **Bathing—No Slipping:** Put a rubber mat on the bottom of the tub. It will prevent the dog from slipping and feeling out of control.

• **Bathing—Ear and Eye Preparation:** Gently put a cotton ball in each ear to protect it from water, and put a drop of castor oil in each eye to protect it from soap.

• **To Dry Clean:** Work baking soda into your dog's dry coat and brush it out thoroughly. It should remove dirt and eliminate dog odor.

• **To Remove Skunk Smell:** Put on rubber gloves, then rub tomato juice, watered-down ketchup, or white vinegar into the dog's coat. Follow up with a bath—heeding all of the (above) BATHING tips: baking soda, rubber mat, cotton balls, and castor oil drops. Or start out by giving the dog a bath, to which you add a box of baking soda, the juice of a couple of lemons, and a dollop of human shampoo.

• **Stop Nonstop Shedding:** Once every ten days or two weeks, massage olive oil or lanolin into your dog's coat. In addition, feed her three egg yolks a week. The added lubrication should control the shedding, and you should see a healthier-looking coat on the dog within weeks.

• **Loose-Hair Remover:** Hook the small upholstery-brush attachment to your vacuum cleaner and suck up your dog's just-shed hair while it's still on him. Once he gets used to the noise, he won't mind this treatment.

• **To Clean Dog's Wire Brush:** Slide a toothpick down the first row of bristles, under the dog's hair, then lift it up and clear off the hair. Continue doing this throughout the rows of bristles until the brush is clean.

• **Walking in Snow:** Rock salt and other chemicals used to melt snow can irritate dogs' paws. For relief, they lick their sore paws— chemicals and all—which can make them sick. Protect your dog's paws in the snow with four small plastic sandwich bags secured with rubber bands. If they're too slippery, or if your dog tears them off, cover the bags with a baby's socks, also secured with rubber bands. If that still doesn't work, try ribbed condoms—really!— so that your dog can practice safe walking.

• **Après Snow:** If your dog went out with unprotected paws, wash them afterward with a mixture of one tablespoon baking soda in a cup of water. The solution should soothe the burning caused by rock salt and other chemicals.

• **Snow Without Chemicals:** If you know that your dog is going to romp in snow that has not been salted, spray the bottom of his paws with a nonstick vegetable spray, to prevent snow from packing between his pads.

• **Dry, Cracked Pads:** Apply a little petroleum jelly to lubricate and soothe the dog's dry pads.

• **Doghouse Bedding:** Foam rubber—from an old car seat, for instance—is good bedding for a doghouse. It's soft and comfortable, and little creepy crawlers—like ticks—will not embed themselves in it as they might in cloth bedding.

DOG TRAINING

• **Keep Off!:** Your dog will stop jumping up on the sofa or chair if you put a big piece of aluminum foil across the seat. The noise and glitter will frighten him away. Or put a whoopie cushion under the cushion of the sofa or chair. Talk about a frightening noise . . .

• **To Prevent Chewing Furniture Legs or His Own Paws:** If your dog is chewing on wood or his paws, chances are he's bored. Until you find toys or a mate to divert his attention, put hot chili sauce on furniture legs, then buff it off. On his paws, paint oil of cloves (available at health food stores) to cure him of chewing.

• **To Stop Your Dog from Chasing Cars:** Remember that broom handle you saved? Or was it that old-fashioned plunger handle? At last, a use for it. Cut a piece of the handle the width of your dog, and drill a hole in the middle of it. Tie twine through the hole. The piece of twine should be long enough to attach to the front of the dog's collar and short enough so the piece of wood hangs down to the dog's knees. Walking should be no problem, but when he runs after cars, the stick will get between his legs and he'll trip.

Attach an appropriate length of chain to the front of your dog's collar so that when he chases cars the chain will flog his legs.

• **To Prevent Your Dog from Digging Holes:** Blow up a few small balloons and bury them in the exact spots where your dog likes to dig. When he starts plowing through the dirt and his toenails pop a balloon, chances are he'll no longer have the desire to dig. (This solution is not for an old dog with a heart condition. See the next remedy instead.)

You know those toilet-freshener cakes? Hammer one to bits and spread it over the area your dog likes to dig. The aroma should be too much for her sensitive nose.

PUPPIES

• **Giving Them Away:** When mama dog has a litter, put pieces of cloth—one for each puppy—in her bed. As each puppy is adopted out, give one of those pieces of cloth to the new family to use in the puppy's bed. The familiar scent should keep the pup from crying for its mama.

• **To Keep a Puppy from Crying:** If a piece of cloth didn't come with your puppy (see GIVING THEM AWAY above), there are a few things you can do to comfort your new little frightened friend and help him make it through the night. For instance, keep a ticking clock near him—he'll appreciate the noise. Wrap a hot-water bottle in a soft blanket so he can cuddle up to it, sort of like a rubber surrogate mom. Or put something you've just taken off—a pair of socks, a T-shirt—in his bed. Your scent will give him a sense of security.

During the day, if you go out and leave him alone, let the radio stay on—no hard stuff; some easy-listening station—to keep him company.

FISH

• **Homecoming:** When you bring home a pet fish in a plastic bag with water, before you take the fish out of the bag, put the whole bag—fish included—in your aquarium and leave it there for half an hour, giving the fish time to get used to the tank's water temperature.

• **To Clean a Crusty Tank:** Use a wet nylon pouf with noniodized salt or vinegar and rinse thoroughly. Then rinse again. Never use soap to clean a fish tank.

BIRDS

• **Hummingbird Feeder:** Add red food coloring to the sugar water in the feeder. It will serve two purposes: you'll be able to see when you should replace the "nectar," and you'll get hummingbirds' attention, since they're drawn to the color red. You may want to make it even more attractive by painting a design on the feeder with red nail polish.

• **For Birdcage Location, Keep in Mind:** The kitchen is not a good place for a birdcage. Small birds can get sick—or worse—from kitchen fumes, such as those produced when you burn a nonstick pan. You should also keep a cage away from areas where birds can be

Folk Belief: Bird Beginnings

When a bird's song wakes you up, you're assured of a day

when everything goes right.

exposed to harsh sprays or commercial cleansers like ammonia (none of which are too good for you either). While birds need light and circulating air, they shouldn't be kept in direct sunlight for very long, and they should be a safe distance away from air conditioning or heating ducts and drafts.

• **Parakeet-Talking Teacher:** A woman will probably be more successful in teaching a parakeet to talk because, generally speaking, a female voice is higher pitched and more like that of the bird.

• **Painting a Birdcage:** Be sure to use nontoxic paint.

• **Outdoor Birdbath:** Add colorful marbles to the water to make the bath more inviting.

14

GARDENING

GARDENER'S CLEANLINESS AND COMFORT

• **For Clean Nails Without Gloves:** Dampen a bar of soap and then claw at it with your nails. Get the soap under your nails and keep it there while you garden. The soap will prevent the dirt from creeping in. Once you're finished in the garden, you can easily nail-brush the soap away.

• **Clean Up Outdoors:** Near the garden hose, hang an old, unwearable pantyhose leg with a bar of soap in it. When the barbecued lunch is ready, or if you're through gardening for the day, wash up *outside,* using the soap without taking it out of the stocking. Then rinse with the hose.

• **Knee Protection:** Sew knee patches on old jeans and leave a few inches open on top. Then insert a pair of shoulder pads or insert kitchen sponges to protect your knees.

Ladies, if you're not the *dungaree doll* type, wear a pair of old pantyhose with foam rubber pads slipped in and lined up at the knees.

SEEDS

• **To Store:** Keep seeds in the refrigerator in a tightly closed glass jar with silica gel in it to absorb moisture. Even this year's leftover seeds kept in the fridge will probably be usable next year. In fact, most seeds are able to germinate for two or three years if kept in a cool, dry, bug-free place.

Folk Belief: Gardening

An Indonesian tradition is that when planting a garden you should

stand on the soil with a long blade of grass in hand. Close your eyes and

patiently wait until you hear the song of a happy bird. At that moment,

open your eyes, tie a knot in the blade of grass, and as you do, tie

in it the vision of a fruitful harvest and place the knotted blade

gently into the earth.

• **To Test Large Seeds and Weed Out Duds:** Empty out the seeds into a bowl of water. The fertile seeds will sink; the duds will float.

• **Planting Tiny Seeds:** Mix the seeds with dry sand (available at nurseries, hardware stores, and pet shops). With the help of the sand, the seeds won't be clumped together. Instead, the plants will grow stronger because of the even distribution. Fill a large saltshaker with the seeds and sand to use when planting—it's a neat way to sprinkle them out.

• **Do-It-Yourself Seed Tape:** Place seeds on wax paper in a straight line that's as wide as the transparent tape you're going to use. Then place the tape—sticky side down—over the seeds, lifting them off the wax paper. Of course, you should plan the landscaping before you plant row after row of seeded tape.

FERTILIZER

• **Organic Gardeners' Most Famous Slogan:** Feed the soil, not the plant.

• **Fish Parts:** It is said that Native Americans taught the Pilgrims to use fish as fertilizer. It's still a good idea—if there are no cats around.

Folk Belief: Planting Seeds

Plant three seeds in separate pots at the same time, and for each, imagine

something wonderful you want to have happen. According to folklore,

the order in which the seeds sprout will be the order in which your

wishes will come true.

Collect and freeze unused fish parts (heads, tails, fish from a catch that you prefer not to eat). When it's time to plant, dig holes deeper than you intend to use for planting, and bury the fish. Replace the soil, then plant as usual.

Fish are rich in nutrients—calcium, sodium, phosphorus, potassium, iron (for leafy vegetables)—that dissolve easily.

• **Poultry Bones:** Save the chicken bones that are otherwise thrown out with the bucket, and keep the turkey carcass after the carving. Let the bones dry out, then put them in a recycled burlap bag. When you have enough to sprinkle over the garden, hammer them down (in the bag) to tiny bits and pieces, then distribute them on the soil in your garden—and houseplants, too.

COMPOST

All gardeners know that *compost* is fermented or decomposed vegetable matter that can be returned to the soil to enrich it. Gray Russell, Compost Project Manager at The New York Botanical Garden, enriches us with these compost tips:

• **What Compost Does:** Compost is not strictly a fertilizer. It also helps improve tilth—or the right crumbly texture in the soil—by letting air, water, and nutrients flow to the roots.

• **When to Start a Compost Pile:** Fall is a great time to begin because of the ready supply of leaves. Gather every fallen leaf you can

Folk Belief: Autumn Leaves

When you catch a falling autumn leaf before it touches the ground,

fortune will come to you. After that first leaf, add a month of good luck

for each additional leaf you catch.

find. Stockpile some; they will be perfect *brown* additions to your compost pile next year, too.

• **The Pile's Moisture Level:** Keep the pile only as damp as a wrung-out sponge.

• **For Best Results:** Alternate foot-thick layers of *greens* (plant cuttings, fruit and vegetable scraps, grass clippings if you don't leave them on the lawn) and *browns* (fallen leaves, wood chips, shredded newspaper, straw). Do not use animal products—no meat, fish, bones, fat, etc.

• **To Keep the Balance Right:** Keep in mind that *greens* break down quickly; too much, and the pile can get smelly and wet. *Browns* break down slowly; too much, and the process can take forever.

• **To Let Air In:** Turn compost piles—poke, lift, and drop from each side. It's important to do this and it only takes about five minutes every week or two.

• **For Fastest Decomposition:** Keep your pile three feet square and three feet tall. The more material is cut up, the faster the compost will be ready. CAUTION: Don't rush it. Using compost before it is properly mature can interfere with plant growth.

• **What's Cooking?:** Wendy Gebb of the New York Horticultural Society explains that a compost heap needs to be kept moist. It's a good idea to hose it down now and then because the moisture helps keep everything decomposing. The decomposing (cooking) process keeps the heap heated. That's why when it's cold out, it's not unusual to see a cat lying on top of the heap to keep warm.

• **How to Tell When It's Ready:** Mature compost is dark-colored and smells earthy. If compost is still hot, it isn't ready yet. Keep it cooking.

• **For Use on the Lawn:** Screen compost into your wheelbarrow and spread a thin layer on the lawn in late fall.

• **Using Compost as a Mulch in Your Beds:** Make it about three inches thick. Apply in the winter after the ground is frozen to prevent thawing and heaving. Apply in the summer to help prevent moisture loss and keep weeds down.

WATERING THE GARDEN

• **Outdoor Flowers:** The best time to water is early in the morning. The moisture is absorbed by the time the hot afternoon sun would evaporate it. Never water in the evening. Wet leaves overnight make plants more vulnerable to fungal diseases.

• **More Is Better:** It's better to water thoroughly at one time—but less frequently—than often but not enough. A sprinkle here and there will weaken the roots, because it forces them upward. When it comes to watering, it's all or nothing.

• **Flowers in Alkaline Soil:** As a treat to plants that grow best in alkaline soil (see GERANIUMS and HYDRANGEA below), every so often water them with a mild mixture of baking soda in water.

HOSES

• **To Store:** Protect a hose from drying out by storing it away from sunlight. In cold weather, never keep it near a furnace or any other heating source.

• **To Recycle a Hose with Holes:** Sprung some leaks in your hose? Make even more holes in the hose and use it as a sprinkler for the garden and lawn.

Folk Belief: Snail Prophecies

Scatter a thin layer of cornmeal on the floor around a table leg and

place a snail on the cornmeal. As the snail crawls through the meal, it is

supposed to spell out the initial of your future mate's name.

PESTICIDES

• **Slugs and Snails:** Wood ashes sprinkled around plants can help keep these creatures away.

Sprinkle baking soda directly on them. When we asked our source how that will affect the slugs, he replied, "They'll think it's snowing and will head south for the winter."

This tip wins the prize for the unanswered: How in the World Did Someone Discover This? Slugs love beer. Gather a few widemouthed jars and fill each one a third of the way with beer. Put the jars into the ground, the rims almost level with the soil's surface. You don't want to do this in the middle of your garden and attract slugs that were never there before. Instead, scatter the jars on the outskirts of your garden, about fifteen feet away. The slugs will find them, drop in, and drown (leaving their bar bill unpaid). Set these beer traps in early evening, then dispose of them the following morning.

• **Squash Bugs:** If you grow squash (and who doesn't?), cucumbers, or pumpkins, repel squash bugs with the reflected light of heavy strips of aluminum foil placed under the vines. As a bonus, the foil also shields the weeds from the sunlight, thus alleviating the weed problem. It also helps keep the soil moist. And as if that weren't enough, it also seems to make the fruit ripen faster.

• **Caterpillars:** If you have a problem with crawly caterpillars, wrap transparent tape around the stems of your affected plants, and the critters will slide right down.

• **Aphids and Other Insects:** Bugs do not like the smell of mint, which is reason enough to grow mint. If you have mint leaves, spread them around the garden or prepare mint tea and water your plants with it.

• **Ladybugs (AKA Lady Beetles, and Ladybirds):** There are about three or four thousand species of ladybugs in the world. Most are red and black, but there are some orange ones with blue markings. Some have as few as two spots, while the thirteen-spotted lady beetle has, well, you know. Named for "Our Lady" the Virgin Mary, these little male—as well as female—creatures are among the most effective destroyers of aphids (during the average ladybug's lifetime, it devours 5,400 aphids), as well as scale insects and other plant-eating pests. *Put away the insecticide!* And put out the welcome mat for ladybugs.

• **Herbs:** Many herbs have insecticidal powers. Figure out which vegetables, fruits, and flowers you want to plant, then do some homework—uh, gardenwork—on the herbs that may help protect your plants. Here are a few to start you off: If you plant cabbage or cabbage-family vegetables such as Brussels sprouts, broccoli, or cauliflower, plant dill, mint, sage, or thyme, which will repel cabbage moths.

Folk Belief: Ladybug, Ladybug

All you have to do is see a ladybug, and lady luck is yours. If it lands on

you, so much the better. If it lands on you on a Sunday and stays long

enough for you to count to twenty-two, there should be no stopping you

where luck is involved.

If you're single and a ladybug lands on you, pay attention when it flies

away. Your future mate will arrive from that direction.

Onions and garlic planted near lettuce or beans will protect them from aphids. They'll also protect plants from Japanese beetles, and carrot flies.

• **Caution:** If you have a commercial poisonous insecticide for your garden, you should think twice about using it on edible plants, including herbs, flowers like nasturtium, and fruits and vegetables.

• **Natural Insecticide:** Separate the cloves of a garlic bulb and toss them into a blender along with one small onion, two tablespoons cayenne pepper, and one quart water. After blending, pour it into a container and let it steep for an hour. Then mix in one tablespoon liquid soap or detergent and it's ready. Sprinkle the solution around the edges of the garden. If you don't use it up right then and there, refrigerate it in a tightly covered jar for no more than one week.

POWDERY MILDEW REMOVER

Mix ¼ cup baking soda in 2 quarts of water, then spray it wherever there is powdery mildew. The problem is especially prevalent on roses, lilacs, and zinnias.

TOOLS

• **To Spot Them Easily:** Paint or tape the handles of your garden tools Day-Glo colors, and you'll never misplace them again.

• **To Measure How Deep You Dig:** Make rulers out of the handles of your hoe and spade. Start at the bottom, and—accounting for the distance between the tip of the blade and the beginning of the handle—mark off inches with a waterproof pen. You'll appreciate having this measuring gauge in hand.

• **To Clean and Prevent Rust:** Saturate a bucket of sand with used motor oil or machine oil. To clean a tool, dunk it in the sand a few times, then wipe it with a paper towel. Store tools in the bucket overnight, or until next season. The sand will clean them off, while the oil will coat them and help prevent rust.

HARD-SURFACE TRIMMING MADE EASY

When planting on the rim of a driveway, sidewalk, or any paved surface, sit on a skateboard and make the job easier by rolling along as you progress.

SPRING GARDENING TIP

• **Crop Rotation Isn't Just for Farmers:** Crop rotation is just as important in the home garden as in commercial agricultural settings, according to Janet Whippo, gardener in the Demonstration Gardens at The New York Botanical Garden. Since different families of plants deplete the soil of different nutrients, Whippo advises that you change locations every year to help prevent some diseases from recurring. Avoid planting crops in the nightshade family—tomatoes, peppers, eggplants, potatoes—in the same place more often than once every four years. This will help reduce pest problems and give the soil-nutrient balance a chance to recover.

EARLY SPRING PLANTING

• **Provide Protection:** Use plastic water, milk, or juice jugs to help plantlets survive a late frost and the ravages of hungry animals. Cut off the bottoms of gallon-size jugs and plant the jugs over the little plants, pushing them about three or four inches into the soil. Keep the caps off during the day. If it gets very cold in the evening, you can put the caps on or throw a cloth over each jug without worrying about crushing the little plants.

TIPS FOR SPECIFIC PLANTS

AFRICAN VIOLETS

• **To Grow Them Bigger, Better, and Healthier:** Sink a few rusty nails in the soil near the growing plants.

APPLE TREES

• **Is It Ripe Yet?** Take an apple off the tree with a clockwise twist. If the apple comes right off, it is ripe. If you twist and twist until the apple *finally* comes loose, allow the other apples more time to ripen.

Check for ripeness by the color of an apple's seeds:

dark brown = ripe;

pale tan or white = not ripe yet.

AZALEAS

• **To Fortify Them:** Azaleas love acidic soil, so give them an occasional cocktail of two tablespoons white vinegar and a quart of water.
• **Hardiest of Them All:** The white azalea stays in bloom longer than any other color azalea.

CABBAGE

• **To Keep Animals from Nibbling:** Sprinkle cayenne pepper on the growing cabbage. After each rainfall, sprinkle again.

Folk Belief: Apple Seed

You're going on a long journey . . . or not. Apple seeds are said to let you know whether you'll travel in the next year. Place a seed on each of your eyelids, assigning travel to one lid and home to the other. Then blink. Keep blinking until one of the seeds falls off. The seed that stays on longest augurs what will come to pass. If the travel seed stays on, start packing; if the home seed stays on, remember, be it ever so humble . . .

• **Two for the Price of One:** If, after cutting off the first mature head of cabbage, you leave the rest of the plant as is, a few more small heads will grow in the same place as the one you just removed.

CORN

• **To Test an Ear for Ripeness:** Gently peel back the husk until about two inches of kernels are showing. With your fingernail, press a kernel until it opens and oozes. If the juice that comes out is milky, the corn is perfect for picking. If the juice is watery, put the husk back the way it was and give it a few more days. If the juice is pasty, tsk, tsk, tsk, the corn is getting too starchy. Remember that corn will be at its prime for only a few days, so start testing about fifteen days after the silk appears.

• **The Time to Pick Corn:** The sugar content is highest late in the day, so pick them in time for dinner. (They taste best when cooked and eaten the same day.)

FERNS

• **To Grow Ferns Faster and Stronger:** Dissolve a birth-control pill—yes, you read correctly—in a quart of water and use it to water the ferns.

A layer of coffee grounds on top of the soil will help a potted fern thrive.

Folk Belief: Corn Luck

To have prosperity in the coming year, hang a bunch of ears

of dried corn on your front door before Thanksgiving.

Folk Belief: Onion Forecasting

Onion farmers can gauge the severity of the season by the

condition of their produce:

Onion's skin very thin,

Mild winter coming in.

Onion's skin thick and tough

Coming winter cold and rough.

GERANIUMS

• **To Help Them Thrive:** Add a layer of rinsed coffee grounds on top of the soil.

HERBS

• **For the Richest Flavor:** Harvest herbs right before the flowers open.

HYDRANGEA

• **To Predetermine Color:** If the hydrangea bush is grown in acid soil, the flowers will be blue; if grown in alkaline soil, they will be pink. In the spring, add aluminum sulfate to the soil for blue flowers, lime for pink.

LETTUCE

• **To Prolong the Harvest Season:** Plant lettuce near a tall-growing vegetable. It will give the lettuce shade, thus keeping it cool and preventing bitterness.

• **To Keep Animals from Nibbling:** Sprinkle cayenne pepper on growing lettuce. After each rainfall, sprinkle again.

ONIONS

• **To Prevent Worms:** Collect used coffee grounds and let them dry. When planting onions, layer the bottom of each row with the dry coffee grounds.

PEAS

• **A Good Reason to Plant 'em:** Planting peas and other legumes is beneficial because they have the power to feed the soil.

• **Friends and Foes:** Beans, carrots, cucumbers, radishes, potatoes, and corn are good company for the pea patch. Keep onion and garlic away from peas, though, because they can inhibit their growth.

PINEAPPLE

• **To Plant a Pineapple:** Slice off the top of the fruit about two inches down from the crown. Let it sit in a bowl of water until the

Folk Belief: Peas, Please

According to legend, peas and sweet peas planted on the night of Saint Patrick's Day will grow abundantly and healthily.

roots seem ready to take root in soil. Plant it in rich, moist potting soil and keep it in bright, indirect light and give it lots of water. In springtime, you may want to take it outdoors.

RASPBERRIES

• **Picking Time:** Since fruit that is dry is less perishable than fruit that is wet, wait until the morning dew is gone before picking raspberries.

• **To Store:** If you collect just-picked raspberries in one big container, the bottom layer will be mush. Instead, use many shallow containers as it takes to gather the harvest without mashing the little fellas on the bottom.

ROSES

• **A-Peeling Nutrients:** Cut banana peels into pieces and bury them around rosebushes just below the surface of the soil (about three peels per rosebush). The calcium, magnesium, phosphorus, potash, sulfur, sodium, and silica derived from the peels will do wonders for the flowers.

• **A New-Growth Booster:** In May and June, in addition to the usual monthly sustenance, give each rosebush one tablespoon Epsom salts. It's rich in magnesium, an element that helps boost the metabolism (rate of growth) of rosebushes.

Folk Belief: Red-Rose Fertility

According to folklore, a woman who wants to conceive

should dry a red rose, grind it into sachet, and wear the sachet in a

little pouch around her neck.

• **When to Cut Roses:** Roses cut in the evening will last longer than those cut in the morning. Throughout the day, stems store food manufactured by the leaves. By evening, the stems are full and hardy—and just-cut flowers will be, too. If you cut flowers in the morning when there's not much food in the stems, they will not have as much stamina.

• **How to Cut Roses:** Cut the stem above the uppermost five-leaflet branch to assure the abundant regrowth of more roses. Cutting below that branch may cause the new shoot to be flowerless.

• **Thorns:** Removing thorns from the stems of cut roses is said to cut short the life of the flower by up to three days.

SWEET POTATOES

• **To Grow:** Start with an organically grown sweet potato. Select one that looks as if the eyes are ready to sprout. Stick toothpicks in the potato's sides and suspend it in a glass of water, immersing it by about one-third. In a couple of weeks the roots should be substantial enough for the potato to be planted in a pot—and the pot to be placed where there is room for vines to grow. Or, if you prefer a lovely ground cover, instead of planting the potato in a pot, clip off the dozens of shoots, transfer them to shallow boxes (flats), provide them with bright lights, and feed them with fish emulsion. When the seedlings seem hardy enough to be uprooted, transplant them in the garden.

TOMATOES

• **When to Plant:** Plant tomatoes during the warmest part of the day. It may not be a terrific time for you, but it's great for the seedlings—because they won't catch a chill.

• **Good Growing Mates:** It's beneficial to plant carrots, chives, leaf lettuce, nasturtiums, onions, and parsley in the tomato patch. Any or all may stimulate growth, help prevent disease, and even enhance the flavor of the tomatoes. Plant dill nearby, and those dreaded hornworms will stay away. Asparagus will help prevent nematodes (pin-

Folk Belief: Lone Asparagus Luck

If you grow asparagus, do not harvest the entire crop all at once.

Leaving just one in place should bring good luck.

worms, hookworms, roundworms) from getting at these *love apples.* In return, tomatoes help repel the asparagus beetle.

The good-neighbor policy also includes French marigolds, which deter whiteflies and sagebrush, which stimulates tomatoes to produce a pest-repelling chemical.

• **Tomato Patch No-Nos:** Cabbage, fennel, kohlrabi, and potatoes should not be planted near tomatoes. Some plants, like people, bring out the worst in each other. *The Moosewood Garden Book* recommends that you separate these vegetables and herbs.

• **Soil Warmer:** You may want to consider spreading black plastic over the planted soil to keep it warm and moist. Don't forget to make holes in the plastic, and plant the plants through them.

• **For Sweeter-Tasting Tomatoes:** Scatter baking soda around the plants. While keeping insects away, it's said to lower the fruits' acidity, making them taste sweeter.

• **When to Pick Them:** Tomatoes are their sweetest when they have reached full color, so that's when they should be picked. This is about five days after you see the first splash of pink.

• **Same Time Next Year, Different Place:** Tomato plants deplete the soil of magnesium. It's best to plant next year's crop in another section of the garden.

Even for first-time tomato planting, use Epsom salts—one teaspoon in each planting hole. The salts' magnesium sulfate can help grow more and bigger tomatoes.

• **In Case of Frost:** If you want to save tomatoes from a frost, pick them even if they're still green. Bundle up each green tomato in three thicknesses of newspaper. While they won't ripen overnight, they should ripen very nicely in time.

TULIPS

• **To Protect Bulbs from Rodents:** Collect large cans, like the ones from fruit drinks. Chances are the top is off each used can. Turn the can into a cylinder by removing the bottom one, too, and sink the cylinder into the soil, stopping when the rim is at ground level. Take out two-thirds of the soil, place the bulb inside, and fill with soil around the bulb up to the rim. The beauty of this *canning* system is that it keeps out the animals and allows the rain to flow through.

CONTAINER GARDENING

Adam Lifton-Schwerner, Foreman of Gardeners at The New York Botanical Garden, believes that *container gardening* is a way to have fun. A temporary relief from the static in-ground garden beds, it allows you a chance to broaden your plant palette, trying plants without regard for winter survival. Lifton-Schwerner shares some of his container gardening tips here:

• **The Basic Planting Mixture:** It should contain equal parts of perlite, loam, and peat moss. Soilless mixtures can be successful—if they drain well.

• **A Rule for All Containers:** They should have drainage holes.

• **Biweekly Feeding:** Every two weeks, feed with a diluted fertilizer solution.

• **To Dress Up Large Containers:** Save room at the edges for plants that will spill down the sides, such as Helichrysum, Petunia integrifolia, Verbena tenuisecta, alyssum, Felicia amelloids, and nasturtium whirlybird—and get those large containers looking full and opulent.

• **Large-Container Consideration:** Very large containers may pose weight problems on terraces, because they need a lot of soil. By using a thick layer of perlite at the bottom and an inverted flowerpot inside, you can reduce the amount of soil needed to fill the container.

• **Another Option:** Try some houseplants as container plants outdoors. In shade, use prayer plants, indoor ferns, aphelandra, and fittonia.

MOONLIGHT GARDEN

• **To Enjoy Your Garden at Night:** Consider growing flowers that will reflect the moonlight and perfume the air. For starters, plant white shrub roses, fragrant white lilies, and flowering tobacco (Nicotiana alata Grandiflora [Fragrant Cloud]), and add a mix of silver-leaved foliage plants such as lavender, lamb's ears, and artemesias.

LAWN

• **When to Water:** Just as the grass starts to wilt, it's time to water. If you're not sure about the *start of wilting,* then check out the color of the grass. When it changes from bright green to a drab blue-green, get out the hose. If you can't pick up on the subtle color change, take a few steps on the lawn. If you can see your footprints for more than a few seconds, get out the hose.

• **Time of Day to Water:** Water early in the morning, before the hot afternoon sun evaporates a lot of the moisture. Never water the lawn at night. Wet grass overnight is more vulnerable to fungal diseases.

• **How to Water:** Water evenly and gently, and never faster than the soil can drink in the water.

• **How Much Water:** It's better to water less frequently but thoroughly (soaking the soil to at least six inches in depth), than often but not enough. A sprinkle here and there will weaken the roots and make the turf susceptible to you-don't-want-to-know-what. So when it comes to watering, forget the frequent spritzing. Instead, completely quench the lawn's thirst without waterlogging.

• **The Best Time to Mow:** Mow in the very late afternoon—a cool time when the surface is dry—to prevent the mower's blades from sticking.

• **Caution:** Mowing when the ground is soaking wet will leave unsightly tire ruts all over your lawn.

• **To Prevent Tire Ruts:** Heed the CAUTION above. And follow this *precaution:* Start at a different place each time you mow, so you don't keep rolling over the exact same lanes and make permanent tire ruts.

• **Grass Height:** It's less stressful for grass to be mowed often, a couple of inches at a time, rather than heavily chopped at one clip.

When grass is at least three inches high, it helps shade the soil and prevent dry-out. Higher grass also deprives the weeds and crabgrass of sunlight (that's a good thing). Another benefit is that leftover grass clippings—hidden unseen in high grass—eventually decompose, returning nutrients to the soil.

• **Snake in the Grass** (See PROTECTION AGAINST ANIMALS—FLOWER-BED SPREAD below.)

TREES

• **Where to Plant a Tree:** Plant trees far enough from your house so that years from now their roots won't damage the house's foundation.

• **A Major Consideration:** Once you've found the spot to plant a tree, picture it all grown up. Is the tree blocking the sunlight from your sunning area or your garden?

• **To Test the Spot:** Since it's very important that the soil in which the tree will be planted has good drainage, test it by digging a hole and filling it with water. If the water drains completely within ten hours, it passes the test.

• **To Brighten Leaves on a Tree:** Water the soil around the tree with beer.

Folk Belief: Planting a Tree

If a friend stands at your side while you lower the tree into the

ground with both hands, it will thrive.

SIDEWALK WEEDS AND GRASS

• **To Get Rid of Cement Greenery:** Pour full-strength white vinegar on the grass or weeds that grow through sidewalk cracks. Within two days, the plants will expire.

• For instant results, pour boiling hot salted water on the unwanted growth.

• **To Prevent Cement Greenery:** Sweep salt or baking soda into the cracks. This and all of the above remedies should also be effective in getting rid of moss on patio bricks.

BUTTERFLIES

• **To Attract Them to Your Flowers:** Butterflies gravitate toward purple, yellow, orange, and red flowers. They love morning glories, verbenas, cornflowers, coreopsis, zinnias, bee balm, marigolds, phlox, sage, cosmos, thistles, and, of course, butterfly weed. Who wouldn't want butterflies in their garden? These beautiful creatures are like flying flowers.

BEES

• **To Help Keep Them Away:** When gardening, do not wear bright colors; stick to beige and other neutral hues. Common sense will tell you that scented hair spray and perfume—particularly floral scents—will attract bees.

• **A Bee-Free Garden:** Vegetables that are harvested before they flower—beets, cabbages, lettuce, carrots, Jerusalem artichokes—are

Folk Belief: Bees, Please

Bees are said to bring good luck. A bee flying into your house signals

a visitor; a bee buzzing around a sleeping child angurs a happy life.

Folk Belief: Butterfly, Flutter By

On any day, if the first butterfly you see is white, play the lottery or ask for

a raise—luck is with you.

not very attractive to bees. Flowers that fit into that unattractive-to-bees category include chrysanthemums, tulips, forsythia, daffodils, and lilacs.

BIRDS

• **How to Scare Crows:** Cut red, black, or orange cloth or heavy plastic into long, thick strips and tie them to garden posts or stakes. The rustling caused by the wind will keep the crows away.
• **To Shoo Birds:** If birds start feeding on just-planted seeds, tie silver Mylar strips (or any flashy tinsel-type material) onto posts or stakes in the garden and say "*sow* long" for now to your bird problems. As soon as the seeds grow to seedlings, put away the tinsel.

PROTECTION AGAINST ANIMALS

• **In the Garden:** Spread aluminum foil on the ground around the plants.

Folk Belief: When You Wish Upon a Crow

As a crow takes off, make a wish. If the crow does not flap its

wings before it's out of sight, your wish will come true.

• **To Protect Young Trees:** To stop animals from taking bites out of the bark, wrap aluminum foil around the bottom half of young tree trunks and secure it in place with heavy twine.

Ask your local beauty salon for a bag of human hair. Recycle unwearable pantyhose feet by filling them with the hair, knotting them closed, and attaching them to young trees and bushes. Deer, rabbits, and other animals will be scared off when they pick up the hair's scent.

• **Flower-Bed Spread:** Mothballs in the soil around plants and shrubs will repel dogs, cats, squirrels, and snakes, too.

If you sprinkle some cayenne pepper on the soil, or a little on the plants, it will send cats, dogs, rabbits, squirrels, and other furry pests running in the opposite direction.

• **Flower Box and Pot Protection:** Pinecones placed around the plants are an attractive way to keep your cat from harming the plants.

• **Keeping Strays Away:** (Be sure to wear rubber gloves for this process—and whenever else you handle hot peppers—and make a conscious effort *not* to touch your eyes. In fact, it's a good idea to put on some sunglasses or goggles.) Toss a few cloves of garlic and a few hot peppers in the blender. Add the mixture to a bucket containing a quart of water. Finish off the concoction with ½ teaspoon dishwashing liquid. Now mark your territory with it: pour or spray it around the edges of your property—both lawn and sidewalk. And remember, this is a temporary deterrent. You'll have to repeat the process after each rainfall.

• **Raccoon Repellent:** Invest in a couple of portable radios. Set them on different talk-radio stations, put each in a plastic bag, and leave them in your garden, creating surroundsound near your almost-ripe produce, such as corn. Remember, it must be *talk* radio; music might *encourage* raccoons to stay for dinner and dancing.

(Also see PROTECTING PLANTS in Chapter 13, "Pets").

DIG IN, CHILDREN

• **To Cultivate a Child's Interest in Gardening:** Michael Levine, Family Garden Coordinator at The New York Botanical Garden, shares his expertise with us. First, he cautions not to overwhelm

Folk Belief: Sunflowers

For many gardeners south of the border, sunflowers are thought

to bring luck. In parts north of the border, the seeds are gathered

at sunset and eaten to ensure a wish come true.

a child with a large garden plot. Instead, start by setting aside a plot that's no bigger than four square feet as the child's very own. Let your child know that, as guardian of that plot, she is responsible for what happens there. As parent and senior gardener, your job is to provide planning and guidance in the form of suggestions, not rules.

Levine recommends that you tap into your child's infinite enthusiasm and wonder—and then follow it. Build bean tepees, make earthworm compost bins, grow flowers. Let your child experiment, have fun, and get lost in the joy of making plants part of her life. The associated memories will last a lifetime.

• **What to Grow:** Michael Levine says that the biggest and fastest-growing are the best for child-size hands—and attention spans. Peas, beans, corn, and sunflowers are the easiest to handle. Radishes provide a crop in only thirty days—with the added buried-treasure appeal of producing a harvest that needs to be unearthed. Lettuce and spinach are good spring crops ready to harvest in fifty days. Strawberries are humble little plants that can be tucked in almost anywhere for a delicious summer treat. And no garden should be without a few plants of Sweet 100 Plus or Sun Gold—prolific, sugar-sweet cherry tomatoes just perfect for popping straight into hungry mouths.

• **For Garden Sprouts (Three-to-Five-Year-Olds):** At The New York Botanical Garden's Ruth Rea Howell Family Garden, Michael Levine starts youngsters with a small area such as a raised-bed container garden. He suggests you try a window box of flowers or pots of mint, parsley, and chives. Everything about gardening should be fun, even the container. Levine uses old shoes and boots, broken watering cans—almost anything that children can identify with. Just remember to punch some holes in the bottom for drainage.

CUT FLOWERS

• **When to Cut Budding Flowers:** Since tightly closed buds may never open in a vase and fully bloomed blossoms won't last very long, pick buds that are about to open or have just opened.

• **Before Plunging into Water:** Cut the stems with a sharp tool, such as a knife or a pair of garden scissors. (A dull pair of scissors might pinch the stems closed.)

Always cut the stems on a slant. That way, the flowers can drink water freely, even when the stems rest on the bottom of the vase. To further help the intake of water, shave off a thin layer of stem lengthwise about an inch from the bottom. For woody stems (lilacs, chrysanthemums, dogwood), scrape and split the ends of the stems. Once you have prepped the stems, place the flowers in water ASAP. Remove all leaves that are below water level so that they don't poison the water.

• **Daily Care:** Put the vase under the faucet and let tepid water run until most of the old water is forced out and replaced by new water. If the floral arrangement is too unwieldy to place under a faucet, use a turkey baster to take out the old water and replace it with fresh lukewarm water. Keep the water level high, just below the rim of the vase. (Incidentally, a baster is also convenient when it comes to watering a Christmas tree.)

Remove flowers and leaves that are clearly goners.

• **Worth-a-Try Life Extenders:** Fill a vase with a quart of warm water, and add two tablespoons white vinegar and two tablespoons sugar. The vinegar suppresses the growth of bacteria, and the sugar feeds the flowers.

Pour some lemon-lime soda or 7UP into a vase of flowers. It seems to perk them up.

Add a teaspoon of salt to the water.

Add a thin slice of soap to the water.

Short-stemmed flowers will thrive in a container of water-saturated sand.

• **Flowers and Fruit:** Do not place fresh flowers near a bowl of fruit. Apples, pears, and bananas emit ethylene gas that can prove deadly to the flowers.

• **Refrigeration:** You probably think that by refrigerating a corsage you will enable it to live longer . . . after all, florists keep flowers re-frigerated. True. But they don't have *fruit* in their refrigerators. As you may have read (above), apples, pears, and bananas give off an eth-ylene gas that will destroy flowers. Eat the fruit, then put the flowers in the fridge, or wrap the flowers in plastic so that the gas can't get at them.

• **Floral CPR:** An aspirin or two can revive wilting blossoms.

Cutting the stems again and placing them in hot water may give fading flowers a second wind.

Put tired flowers in a dark room for an hour, then watch them perk up when they see the light of day.

• **To Prevent Odors:** After a day or two in water, stems—particu-larly thick ones—begin to decay, and with it comes a terrible smell. Prevent this by putting a piece of activated charcoal in the water.

• **To Color Flowers:** If you want to mess with Mother Nature, add food coloring to the water in which you put white or light-colored flowers. As the stems absorb the liquid, the flowers will take on their new color.

CARE OF SPECIFIC CUT FLOWERS

• **Carnations:** Add a little boric acid to the water to add days to their life.

• **Chrysanthemums:** Sugar water in the vase will help them stay fresh longer.

• **Daffodils:** Before you integrate daffodils with other flowers, put them in quarantine. First cut the stems at an angle, then place them in a vase half filled with lukewarm water. In an hour or two (after they've had enough time to release their saplike fluid, which can poison other flowers), spill out that water, and you can safely include the daffodils in a floral arrangement.

• **Gardenias:** Handle these sweet-smelling blossoms with care. Their petals bruise easily.

When entertaining, float gardenias in a bowl as a centerpiece and/or float them in the bathtub.

• **Marigolds:** To help prevent their disagreeable stench, add a teaspoon of sugar or activated charcoal to the water.

• **Rosebuds:** To speed up the blossoming process, add a teaspoon of sugar to the water.

• **Tulips:** A copper penny in the water should help keep them from opening too wide and flopping over.

FLOWER ARRANGING

• **Flower Holder:** A lattice berry container turned upside down and placed on the bottom of a vase is a great help when arranging flowers.

Put transparent tape across the mouth of a vase, and it will help you place flowers exactly where you want them in an arrangement. Crisscross two lengths of tape, or do it tick-tack-toe style—whatever works for the size of the vase's opening and the flowers you plan to put in it.

• **When Stems Are Too Short:** Lengthen flowers by placing each stem in a clear drinking straw. Then cut the straws to the ideal length for the vase.

If you're not going to make the stems longer, then make the vase seemingly shorter by layering the bottom with marbles.

• **Creative Containers:** Dare to be different. Use that dented old teapot in your giveaway box; your ex-husband's tennis trophy cup in the garage; the horseradish jar in the recycle bin; hey, the recycle bin!

DRIED FLOWERS

• **A Drying Process:** Take into consideration the size and number of flowers you want to dry, and use an appropriate container in which to combine ten parts white cornmeal and three parts borax. Gently bury the flowers in the mixture. Keep it out of harm's way, and, after two weeks, carefully uncover the dried flowers.

• **Another Drying Process:** When you want to dry a bouquet of flowers, tie string around the stems, turn them upside down and let them hang that way in a cool, dark place until they've completely dried. If you take the leaves off before you start the drying process, you'll save yourself the trouble of picking them up once they've dried and fallen off.

This method of drying works better with some flowers than others. Our favorites are baby's breath, heather, hydrangea, statice, sunflower, and yarrow.

HOUSEPLANTS

• **Pollution-Fighting Plants (NASA Knows Best):** Indoor air contaminants are inescapable. They come from furniture, drapes, carpets, insulation, household cleaning agents, paint, office machines, paper towels, facial tissues, inks, plastics . . . just about everything!

The National Aeronautics and Space Administration conducted extensive research and found five common, attractive, and easy-to-grow houseplants that can dramatically reduce toxic chemical levels. Yes, you can clean the air you breathe by placing any or all of the following plants in your home and office.

• **Spider Plant:** Very easy to grow in indirect or bright, diffused light.

• **Peace Lily:** Very easy to grow in low-light location.

• **Chinese Evergreen:** Very easy to grow in low-light location.

• **Weeping Fig (Ficus benjamina):** Fairly easy to grow but requires a little special attention. Needs indirect or bright, diffused light.

• **Golden Pothos:** Very easy to grow in indirect or bright, diffused light.

• **NASA's Recommendation:** One plant will remove up to 87 percent of toxic organic pollutants in a hundred-square-foot area. A plant in each room should be adequate.

Once the plants are in place, don't be surprised if problems caused by contaminants—sore throat, stuffy nose, teary eyes, headaches, skin eruptions, nausea—completely disappear.

• **When to Bring Home Houseplants:** Francisca Planchard-Coelho, gardener at The New York Botanical Garden, suggests that you wait until April to introduce new houseplants. When the light becomes stronger and the days are longer, there will be fewer problems.

• **When to Water:** Gardener Planchard-Coelho suggests that you water when it is warmer, not colder, in the house—in the morning after you turn on the heat.

• **How to Water:** Regular-but-light sprinklings will weaken the roots. Water less often—once a week or whenever plant is dry—but more thoroughly. Plants prefer lukewarm water. Never use ice-cold water.

• **For Overwaterers:** Get plants that thrive in water. The following will grow for at least a year in a vase kept out of direct sunlight: Chinese evergreen, pothos (both part of NASA's list of depollutants), coleus, grape ivy, and wandering Jew.

• **Fortifying Tonics:** Dissolve an aspirin in a cup of tea, and water your plants with it once a month. If you have an aquarium, when you change the water, don't pour the old water down the drain. Instead, water your plants with it. They'll love it!

Next time . . . *every* time . . . you steam or cook vegetables, save the vitamin-packed water as a treat for your plants.

Next time . . . *every* time . . . you hard-boil eggs, save the water and water your plants with it. If you're big on hard-boiled eggs, toss eggshells into a container with water and leave them for a few days, then use that water to nourish your plants.

For a nitrogen boost, dissolve a packet of unflavored gelatin in a quart of water to water your plants once a month.

• **To Increase Humidity:** Planchard-Coelho advises that you place houseplants and orchids on trays of pebbles with water, but keep the plants above the water level.

• **Illuminate Sunlight:** For plants that need all the light you can provide—such as geraniums, weeping fig, jade plant, and cacti—line the windowsill with aluminum foil. The plants will appreciate the additional reflected light.

• **To Brighten Leaves:** Serve plants sodium-free club soda or seltzer (which is always sodium-free) that has gone flat, and the color of the leaves should become more vivid.

• **To Clean and Shine Leaves:** Wash your plants with a mixture of ¼ cup baking soda and 2 quarts water with a sponge or cloth, one leaf at a time.

Leaves will look their greenest after a gentle massage with mineral oil or castor oil.

• **Coasters for Flowerpots:** Use self-sticking corn pads or bunion pads on the bottom of flowerpots to prevent surface scratches.

• **After Summering Outdoors:** Move houseplants into shade a week before bringing them indoors for the winter, says Dora Galitzki, Plant Information Specialist at The New York Botanical Garden, who also recommends that you check those plants and pots for hidden insects.

• **Pesticide:** Next time you water your bug-plagued plant, add a few drops of liquid detergent to the water. The little buggers will go into the soil at night and won't live to come out.

• **To Eliminate Mealybugs:** If you see little cottonlike puffs on stems and leaves, your plant has mealybugs. Get rid of them by dabbing each puff with a cotton swab dipped in alcohol. If the problem has spread and your plants are overrun with 'em, spray with a mixture of equal parts of alcohol and water. Don't take any chances: give it a week, then spray again.

Since we're sure that you're not foolish enough to smoke, go to a hotel lobby and collect the cigarette butts from the stand-with-the-sand. Take out the tobacco and soak it in water for twenty-four hours. Strain out the water into a spray bottle and give those mealybugs a good spritzing. They will be living proof that cigarettes can kill ya'!

REPOTTING PLANTS

• **Drainage:** When replanting houseplants, recycle Styrofoam packing pellets by using them for drainage. They're lightweight and sturdy—a fine combination for layering under soil.

Nylon net, the kind of bags onions come in, can be used for drainage under soil.

• **Stop Soil Leakage:** When repotting, the first thing you may want to put in the pot is a coffee filter. The filter will prevent just-watered soil from seeping out the drainage hole and soiling the saucer.

HANGING PLANTS

• **Watering:** It's often suggested that you can avoid the hassle of climbing up to water hanging plants by putting ice cubes on the soil, and as the ice cubes melt, the plant is watered. We're here to tell you that the idea sounds great, but it's not great for the plant. Check out HOW TO WATER (above), and you'll understand why watering with ice cubes leaves us cold.

• **To Prevent a Mess of Drips:** Before you give your hanging plant a good and proper watering, place a shower cap over the bottom of the hanging container. Leave it there long enough to catch all the dirty drips after the watering. Good luck removing the cap without spilling a drop!

FLOWERING PLANTS

• **For Bountiful Blossoms:** The roots of flowering plants need to be *squished in* a pot rather than *spread out*. Make sure they are not in pots that are too big for their own good.

• **To Clean:** At least once a week wipe large-leaf plants with a damp cloth; spray small-leaf plants with a mister; clean fuzzy-leaf plants (including cacti) with a soft brush.

• **To Encourage a Young Plant:** Use your fingers to pinch off the growing tips of stems. This tip-snipping will result in the growth of lower-down dormant buds. This is a good thing, because you want a plant to grow *out* more than *up,* or *full* and *bushy* rather than *long* and *scrawny.* Never pinch a palm, or any other one-point-of-growth plant. Vines? Yes, pinch away for bushier vines.

• **As Flowers Start to Wither:** Remove them to prevent the plant from using its energy to produce seeds.

GARDENING BY ZODIAC

Folk wisdom and astrologists claim that your birth sign influences the type of garden you should grow. Thanks to the experts at *Flower Gardens* magazine, here is planting information to help gardens grow better with specific guidance under each gardener's sign of the zodiac:

AQUARIUS (JANUARY 21–FEBRUARY 19)

Your best color is blue. Plan a garden that includes lots of blue and lavender flowers, and it will bring you great joy. Plants you should try are bachelor buttons, blue delphiniums, and forget-me-nots. Climbing vines will grow especially well for you.

Wednesdays are your best day. For best results in weeding and sowing, be sure to use part of this day for garden chores.

PISCES (FEBRUARY 20–MARCH 20)

Pisces is a water sign—auspicious for gardeners. Your best color is violet. If you have never raised violets, you should try them. Yours are liable to be prizewinners. Plants that prefer moist, damp conditions will do well for you. Consider digging a small pond or pool for water lilies. Try something exotic and plant a lotus (perhaps in a Japanese garden?).

Friday is your lucky day—that's the day to plant. Some gardeners dream of formal gardens with row after row of neat plants, but not you! Casual borders with flowers spilling over a country path are much more your style.

ARIES (MARCH 21–APRIL 20)

Bold Aries people love dramatic gardens full of hot tropical colors. But be careful—your boldness can be your undoing. Many Aries people make ambitious plans for their gardens during their birth month and start out with energy and self-confidence, only to scale back their plans dramatically as spring turns to summer.

Red and orange blossoms are most attractive to you. For some reason, you also have an affinity to delicate cup-shaped yellow and white jonquils. You'll successfully grow many spring-flowering bulbs to perfection.

TAURUS (APRIL 21–MAY 21)

Those born under the sign of Taurus the Bull have particularly fruitful natures. Even Taureans cooped up in apartment houses are able to demonstrate their skill through window boxes and container gardens. Their office plants thrive while others wither and die. Take heart, city Taureans, when you retire, you'll probably find that place in the country you've always dreamed about.

Your color is yellow, and your flower is the sweet pea. Your lawn will be its best if you tend it on Monday or Friday.

GEMINI (MAY 22–JUNE 21)

Geminis are filled with energy, which makes them truly terrific gardeners. Unfortunately, their excess energy makes them impatient, which means they sometimes plant too soon or get bored waiting for the garden to flower. Here's a hint: find another hobby to go with your gardening. Your dual nature, and great gardening skills, will allow you to do both. Try painting or photographing your flowers. Enter garden-club contests, and blue ribbons will likely be yours.

Your best flower is the lily-of-the-valley.

CANCER (JUNE 22–JULY 23)

Your planet's ebbs and flows affect you tremendously. Be careful of enthusiasm that is overwhelming one day and nonexistent the next. The ups and downs make it hard for you to get started on a garden. On the other hand, you are a water sign—which is unusually fertile—so if you can get it together, your garden is likely to succeed. And once it gets started, you'll know what you need to do.

If you can, situate your garden near a small creek. Otherwise, any source of water will do. Without water, you will always feel that your garden is missing something. Animals seem to be attracted to your yard. Enjoy them! They come to be near you. Your best flower is the rose.

LEO (JULY 24–AUGUST 23)

Those born under the sign of Leo the Lion are leaders and teachers, and, hopefully, this applies to you. Work with others to help them acquire gardening skills, and you will reap great rewards. Perhaps at your child's school or a nearby senior citizen center? Your gift is not complete unless it is shared.

Your ruling planet is the sun—another clue to your gardening ability. Make room for sunflowers in your garden. Your best flowers are gold or bright yellow.

VIRGO (AUGUST 24–SEPTEMBER 23)

Virgos tend to be independent yet practical people. Build your garden in your own way. Virgo gardens are easy to maintain and excite the envy of their neighbors. It's a lot easier for you to follow a garden plan year after year than to change plantings. If you are starting an herb border where nothing has ever grown before, it will surely succeed.

Use color—lots of color. Virgos have an affinity with gladiolas and hyacinths. Your independent nature means you'll rarely need help in your garden. But be generous with your time to help others with their gardens.

LIBRA (SEPTEMBER 24–OCTOBER 23)

Whether they know it yet or not, Libras have green thumbs. Sometimes, however, they spend years thinking about gardening before getting the courage to actually start one. Once you do start one, watch out! You'll be hooked for life.

Libras tend to have gardens that are artfully arranged and carefully planned. Few allow their creations to be diminished or destroyed through lack of care. Your best flower is the aster, and your lucky day is Friday.

SCORPIO (OCTOBER 24–NOVEMBER 22)

Scorpios are famous for being passionate and intense, traits that are frequently found in the finest gardeners. Once you set your mind to something, you'll get the job done with a minimum of difficulty. Be careful, though—your competitive nature can sometimes get you into trouble, especially with your neighbors.

Scorpios are born under a fertile sign and love the colors purple and red. Flowers with many petals do best under your guidance.

SAGITTARIUS (NOVEMBER 23–DECEMBER 21)

Sagittarians are warm and generous people, always willing to help others. Be careful, though—you sometimes help out all of your neighbors at the expense of your own garden. Think a minute before you lend out your favorite tools, because others may not treat them with the same respect you do.

Your best flower is the chrysanthemum. Try some of the more exotic new hybrids. Purple flowers will please you beyond all others. Dark clematis, rich heliotrope, and jewel-tone iris are good choices.

CAPRICORN (DECEMBER 22–JANUARY 20)

Quiet and determined, Capricorns are particularly respectful of our Mother Earth. Capricorns honor tradition and tend to plant old-fashioned favorites or heirloom flowers in gardens planned in old-fashioned ways.

Your best color is green, which is why foliage plants have a special effect on you. Choose ones with mottled leaves, bicolored leaf margins, or dramatically shaped leaves to enhance your beds. Your best flower is the narcissus, which isn't surprising, since your birthday falls around the time when they should be forced into bloom.

INDEX